THE SECRETARIAL GHETTO

THE
SECRETARIAL
GHETTO

by Mary Kathleen Benét

McGraw-Hill Book Company
New York   St. Louis   San Francisco

THE SECRETARIAL GHETTO

Copyright © 1972 by Mary Kathleen Benét.

First edition in the United States of America 1973.

07–004536–4

123456789BPBP79876543

First printed in Great Britain by Sidgwick and Jackson.

Library of Congress Cataloging in Publication Data

Benét, Mary Kathleen.
  The Secretarial Ghetto

  Includes bibliographical references.
  1. Secretaries. 2. Woman—History and condition of
women. I. Title.
HF5547.5.B42 1973   331.4'81'6513741   72–10053
ISBN 0–07–004536–4

AUTHOR'S NOTE

AN EXAMINATION of what has been written on the "woman question" for the last century shows that today's offices are far from unique in their treatment of women, and that all the questions raised by women's subsidiary role have been debated again and again. The positions taken by today's feminists are not new, although they are now expressed in the rhetoric of left-wing politics.

Interviews with several hundred secretaries supplemented the reading that went into this book. Offices in the United States and Europe yielded a story of discontent that was hotly challenged by the bosses, personnel managers, and employment agents whose views were also sought. Sometimes it was hard to believe that the two sides were talking about the same offices. The views expressed by secretaries in all situations and all countries were remarkably similar, as were the men's opinions. It seemed, finally, that there really was a sex war going on in the office, and that it bore some similarity to a class war—but with a female proletariat and a male capitalist class.

M.K.B.

CONTENTS

0533870

THE SECRETARIAL GHETTO

Chapter One
INTRODUCTION

THE OFFICE TODAY is a female ghetto. In the Western world it is by far the largest single employer of women. Six out of ten American office workers are female, and the vast majority play secretarial roles: answering phones, making coffee, endlessly performing the mind-numbing paperwork of bureaucracy.

Secretaries today stand at the crossroads of two revolutions, which may change their lives irrevocably. One of these movements is the revolt of the white-collar worker, who sees his privileged status being eroded and his standard of living falling. The other is Women's Liberation.

It has been an article of feminist faith that when women achieved the right to work, their economic independence would inexorably lead to equality in every sphere. But women in offices act out the roles that women have always played—those of wives, mothers, and mistresses. Their work is supplementary and custodial rather than productive: it is low in status and in pay.

Women's liberationists have blamed men and "the system" for this, as they have for other aspects of women's oppression. But they have also blamed the office women themselves, calling them sell-outs and collaborators. The secretaries, cheered on by their bosses, have reacted with increased loyalty to the status quo.

In fact, the situation is more complicated than either side is willing to admit. It has deep historical and psychological roots. A comparison of male and female attitudes towards the secretary's job reveals some of the problems that any office revolutionary will have to tackle.

The ten commonest male comments:

1. (leer) *Must be a fascinating subject!*
2. *My secretary knows my job better than I do.*
3. *My secretary likes her job.*
4. *Wish I could get a job anywhere I liked, the way these girls can.*

5. *Girls come here asking about the executive-training program, and they can't even type.*
6. *I've got all the junior executives I need, but even for $155 a week, I can't find a secretary.*
7. *A girl who isn't likely to get married and leave wouldn't fit in around here.*
8. *Who needs someone who glares at you every time you ask her to do some typing?*
9. *I really ought to hire an older woman.*
10. *Someone's got to do it.*

1. (leer) *Must be a fascinating subject!*
The first thing that comes to many a man's mind when he thinks about secretaries is sex. The media share his obsession—the questions raised about secretaries are: Is she sleeping with the boss? How sexily should she dress on the job? Men in offices speculate endlessly about the girls, comparing them, picking favorites, teasing them. In fact, most office men will tell you that that's why the girls are there.

The sexual roles that women play in "real life" have been transferred to the office, where they are ritualized like all the rest of office behavior. Having a chic, charming receptionist is as much of a status symbol as having an elegant wife. Dictating to a pretty young thing is as satisfying to the male ego as dominating her sexually would be. And being coddled and taken care of by an efficient secretary is as good as going home to Mother.

The important question isn't really whether the boss is sleeping with his secretary, although he may be. The mime that's acted out in the office is, as in a Bunny Club, more concerned with appearance than reality, and is all the more satisfying for that reason. No demands are made on the man; he can indulge his fantasies without having to perform.

Every aspect of secretarial life is explored by the newspapers in sexual terms. One article reports that open-plan offices are discouraging bottom-pinchers; another asserts that temporary work is being used by girls for concentrated husband-hunting. Even the Pill is good copy: it's thought to have made attendance more reliable and to have removed the risk of a secretary vanishing in mid-memo to have a baby.

In part, all this reflects the fact that women are still thought of first as sexual beings, not as workers. No amount of work on their part seems to dispel this assumption. No wonder, for it has been embedded in our thinking right from the days of Dr. Spock, who says: "In our kind of society we believe that the frustrated desire of boys to make a baby becomes part of men's urge to create things: buildings, bridges, machines, inventions, books, plays, music and pictures."[1] With this kind of justification, the woman bridge-builder can be told, "Why do you need to do that? You can make babies instead." The implication is "Lucky you," which makes her seem perverse as well as unnatural if she insists that a bridge is what she really wants to make.

This argument is more basic than any of the other debates about women: how long mothers are needed at home, how the economy can use female labor, how much housework is really necessary, and so on. These questions would be easy to solve once people made up their minds whether the need for productive work is sex-linked.

2. *My secretary knows my job better than I do.*

This is the "power behind the throne" argument, as insincere today as it has been throughout history. He doesn't really believe it; if he did, it would be the one thing he would be anxious to suppress. He can say it, with every appearance of gallantry, because no one is going to take him seriously.

The easiest way to expose his insincerity is to ask, "If she's so good at your job, why are you still around?" Then the answers range from "She doesn't really have the training" to "The clients would never deal with a woman."

Complimenting his secretary is one way for an executive to boost his own importance. If he needs a capable, intelligent girl to back him up, what he's doing must be pretty crucial. He must be so busy that he can't possibly keep all the details of his job in mind. He must also be indispensable; someone always has to be in his office to answer questions and keep track of his whereabouts.

More confident men emphasize the amount of autonomy their secretaries have, and compliment them in such terms as "She answers most of my letters by herself now," or "She's completely taken over the payroll accounting." The implication is that the more he can be freed for pure thought, pure "decision-making," the more valuable he will be to the company. Delegating his routine tasks makes him more, not less, useful.

This line is also used to combat talk about the oppression of secretaries: "What more does she want? She has so much challenge and opportunity right here. I'm only too glad to turn over to her anything she's willing to take on. Do you think I like having to bother myself with all these petty details?"

The crunch comes when the enlightened boss is asked, "What about turning over to her some of the things you *do* want to do, instead of leaving her the boring parts? What about sending her to the management conference in Hawaii while you struggle with the monthly balance sheet? And what about paying her more the more she takes on? You know you wouldn't look at the work itself as reward enough, the way you're asking her to."

The same old arguments come up again: "The board wouldn't stand for it" and "I'm paid to take the responsibility." In other words, "I don't want to." As usual, the secretary's own satisfaction is way down the list of priorities—the only reason it might appear there at all is to keep her from leaving. The boss's satisfaction, however, is right at the top of the list—how can he manage efficiently if he's feeling frustrated, tired, unhappy, or underpaid?

3. *My secretary* likes *her job.*
It's a fact that if you ask secretaries, "Do you like your job?" most of them will answer, "yes." And they'll be annoyed if anyone implies that he (or she) knows better than they do how they really feel about it. So far, the boss is telling the truth.

But the unspoken question behind their answer is "Compared to what?" Most askers of the question mean, would the secretaries rather have more interesting, responsible jobs—their bosses' jobs in fact? And this question really doesn't have much meaning.

The chances are just about nil. The secretary is on a completely different career track from the start, and she knows it. She has long since learned to console herself by making the best of her own niche and convincing herself that she is happy there.

She might well reply, "Since this situation is likely to stay the way it is, why work up a case against it? Why ask for trouble?" Secretaries are so often told how privileged, desired, and envied they are that it seems madness to complain, whatever they may feel like doing.

After all, many secretaries *do* like their jobs whichever way you look at it. For many, perhaps for most, secretarial work has been an avenue into a world they would otherwise never see, and a form of contact with powerful, interesting men they would never otherwise meet. They have risen in the social scale, their pay has been going up faster than the average for the last few years, they dress well and work in comfortable offices. Lots of them are doing just about as well as any woman, anywhere, can expect to do.

The disadvantages of executive life have been pointed out to them by everyone from their mothers to their bosses. Do they really want the ulcers, the long hours, the endless office politics? Many of them can quite honestly say no.

But recognizing all this doesn't put an end to the argument. Maybe the slaves (or some of them) were happy in the old South. It isn't even necessary to say, "Well, if they're happy, they shouldn't be." The question is whether making the best of a bad deal is all the happiness a woman at work can expect. If she expects no more, and thus feels roughly satisfied with what she's got, isn't that a worse comment on the system than any amount of agitation would be?

Another problem for the questioner is that absolute loyalty is demanded of the secretary. She knows that part of what she is paid for is morale—a cheerful, smiling face, comfort in adversity, calm and serenity at all times. She knows that grousing or complaining to an outsider is forbidden. She becomes such a good actress that anyone can be fooled by her—and her boss, who wants to believe that his minions love him, is one of the easiest of all to fool.

4. Wish I could get a job anywhere I liked, the way these girls can.

This is said in the tone of, "I wouldn't mind going on welfare," or "I wish they'd build some low-rent housing for *me*," or even "I'm dying for the day when I can sit at home and send my wife out to work." Lies, every one. He wouldn't really trade places with his secretary, his wife, or anyone on welfare. Watch his reaction when it's suggested that he should share the housework, when he has to type something for himself, or when he gets fired.

The insidious thing about this argument is that, like the previous one, it uses the advantages of the secretary's lot to argue that there are no disadvantages to it. There's *something* to be said for almost anyone's job.

This particular advantage is really the main one secretaries have, and it's the one usually cited by parents urging their daughters to go to secretarial school, by the schools themselves, and by girls trying to plan their futures. All three groups know that whatever else a secretary may be, she is at least employable. Because her function and her training are so general, she can be used almost anywhere in any organization. She can pick up the routine of any office in a matter of hours, and, until she carves out a special niche for herself, she can be replaced just as quickly.

Routine paperwork is probably the fastest-growing activity in the Western world, and, because it was early defined as women's work, women have never been so employable. They can't get paid well and they can't get promoted, but they can at least get hired. It's a good first step.

It is now being argued by some that if women press for higher pay and greater equality at work, they will lose their easy employability. If there's no particular advantage (like cheapness) to hiring women, companies will naturally prefer men. The women shouldn't jeopardize what they have in the effort to get more. Any union worker accused of "pricing himself out of a job" knows the answer to that one, and so, although he often won't admit it, does any ambitious young executive, job-hopping and playing offers against each other in order to climb the ladder. He knows, too, that a seller's market doesn't change just because the sellers put the price up; that's what any sensible seller does while the going is good.

5. *Girls come in here asking about the executive-training program, and they can't even type.*

Gloria Steinem said at a Smith College graduation ceremony that the college vocational office "asks routinely how many words a minute do you type. Harvard and Amherst do not. . . . Perhaps a whole generation of us should fail to learn to type."[2] I would prefer Harvard and Amherst to begin asking the question too. After all, who types their papers? And later on, their letters? Not knowing how to type is like not knowing how to drive or shave yourself.

Those who are destined to fill the top roles in society are trained to use in a wasteful way the labor of those in less "valuable" categories. This habit has almost died out in some areas, like the use of domestic servants; but it persists in the office, where mechanical self-sufficiency is a mark of low status.

Efficiency-conscious organizations are usually the first to dispense with status symbols. Robert Townsend reports in *Up the Organization*, "In my case, unloading a secretary worked out like finding an extra four hours a day."[3] He answers the letters he receives by hand, answers his own phone (asking the switchboard to hold calls if he's busy), and sees people when they want to see him.

Nader and his Raiders don't have secretaries: they all do their own typing. Their efficiency is legendary.

Newspaper reporters are almost the only professional category of American and English men who don't have secretaries. Their tough image means that they don't feel effeminate when they type their own stories. It's a lot faster.

Until all men begin learning from these models, someone else will be doing their typing. And the only recourse for a girl who doesn't want a secretarial job is to refuse to take one.

Another reason for not learning to type is that if a girl really wants to play the corporate game, she ought to learn it as it's really played, which means attaching a lot of importance to status questions like not doing her own typing. Once it is discovered that she really knows how to type, she's suddenly in a different category from the rest of them—and that's fatal.

Not taking secretarial jobs, and refusing to be pushed into them, is a counsel of perfection. Weakening can be forgiven—as long as a girl at least tries to hold out.

6. I've got all the junior executives I need, but even for $155 a week, I can't find a secretary.

Why is it that companies are outraged at having to pay the market price for labor? Secretaries are expensive these days compared to what they used to be; they're still cheap compared to executives. If the supply seems to be dwindling, maybe it's owing to something besides perversity on the girls' part: maybe they aren't being offered a very attractive deal. This logic would be crystal clear to a businessman in any other area, but when he talks about secretaries, a tone of righteous indignation creeps into his voice. "Why aren't the wretches grateful?"

The secretaries aren't all saints nor are the bosses all villains. Many companies throw money down the drain trying to get work out of unwilling, untrained girls, and many offer real opportunities to girls who wouldn't find them anywhere else.

However, I have never seen a woman given a job that's too demanding and responsible for her to cope with—she usually has to prove herself ten times over before being allowed anywhere near it. And I've seen plenty of men struggling with prestigious, high-pressure jobs that really are too much for them. Women aren't challenged enough at work; men are sometimes challenged too much. That's why the turnover rate for women is so high (the biggest cause, by far, of secretarial job-hopping is boredom) and why men have coronaries.

The companies that have trouble attracting and holding secretaries are usually trying to get something for nothing. Either they are paying below the going rate, or they're hiring overqualified girls and treating them unimaginatively. Many companies try to pay in prestige instead of money—all the media are notorious for this. Some are so neanderthal in their methods that life becomes a gray and regimented bore: insurance companies, for instance, often assume that they will get more out of the staff if everything is mechanical and rule-bound. In reality, they are driving people away. Most companies simply don't realize that the expectations of the women they employ are rising fast.

One big change is that more and more women are expecting their own income to support them. They are no longer content to live with their parents until they marry and to be financially dependent on their husbands after that. The divorce and desertion rate these days means that even if they did want to depend on a man, they often can't. The "pin-money" theory of women's work was never as true as employers claimed, but today it is vanishing fast. A hundred and fifty-five dollars a week may be a fortune for a young girl sharing her first flat (although she will have a hard time holding her own in New York), but it's not much for a working mother. It's being asked more and more often why fathers and husbands should subsidize women's employers by allowing them to pay less than the true cost of the women's support. Besides, when, except in the case of women, has pay been determined by "need"?

What the bosses are really complaining about is that they can no longer find someone of high skill for a low wage just because she is a woman. Every woman will applaud this change.

The outcries against secretaries' inflated earnings sound hollow when like is compared with like. A secretary may earn, at the most, about $20,000 in the United States or £4,000 in England, but her fellow office workers, the executives, are on a scale that reaches $768,000 for the chairman of I.T. & T. and £72,809 for the chairman of Shell Transport.

7. *A girl who* isn't *likely to get married and leave wouldn't fit in around here.*
This is the dead giveaway, which shows that most of the myths about working women are self-fulfilling prophecies. Bosses eagerly hire pretty young girls, who happily decorate the place for a few years. When the girl grows bored, there are two alternatives: she can put up with it or she can leave. She can't advance And when a younger girl is hired, the first girl loses the sexual

attention that made the boredom bearable, and so she leaves. The boss claims, "You can't promote women. They'll just leave to get married and have babies."

There are lots of other myths about office girls that operate in the same way. "These little girls never think about anything but clothes and boys." What are they supposed to think about—the filing? "I'm always trying to keep up with what's going on in the firm. My secretary can't see beyond her own little job." He's paid to know what's going on. And if his secretary began taking an interest in the firm as a whole, he would be the first to tell her to mind her own business and get on with the typing. If she has big ideas, her own little job would drive her crazy even faster than it's doing now. Her only hope is to sink herself into numbing routine and stay there. If she has ideas above her station, she's told, "You'll never get anywhere until you've proved yourself in the job you've got." If she doesn't develop ideas above her station, the line is, "How can I promote someone who can't think big?"

Mainly, this remark proves once again that women are admitted to the office as sexual entertainment, not as serious workers. A drab secretary who doesn't have dates may be willing to work late, but who would want her to? She's like an old car—reliable and all broken in, but it's more fun to exchange for a new model every year.

If companies were serious about wanting to reduce turnover, all they have to do is reverse this chicken-and-egg situation. Instead of using turnover as an excuse for no promotion, they could try giving promotions and see how fast the turnover stops; pay women at executive rates and see how quickly they begin behaving like executives: taking work home, coming in even if they have a cold, bullying the typists. Any company that doesn't give these a try isn't really serious about wanting the women to stay around.

8. *Who needs someone who glares at you every time you ask her to do some typing?*
This is usually prefaced by "I'm all for Women's Lib but. . . ." It means, "I don't mind women doing what they want as long as

they continue to do what *I* want, and that includes not only keeping up with the typing, but being cheerful about it—in fact, playing the flirtatious games I like to play around the office."

Most of the outcry against the "unfeminine" liberationists who demonstrate and occupy offices isn't an attack on their looks— they look very much like other girls—but on their refusal to be sexually ingratiating in the traditional way. Shulamith Firestone reports,

> In my own case, I had to train myself out of that phony smile, which is like a nervous tic on every teenage girl. And this meant that I smiled rarely, for in truth, when it came down to real smiling, I had less to smile about. My "dream" action for the women's liberation movement: *a smile boycott,* at which declaration all women would instantly abandon their "pleasing" smiles, henceforth smiling only when something pleased *them.*[4]

The outrage occasioned by an action like this will surprise anyone who tries it. It's part of another double bind commonly practiced in the office. Two remarks are used alternately: "Of course women will never get anywhere if they don't handle people tactfully," and "She's too soft and nice to be a really tough manager."

However, men wouldn't mind a sour face at the filing cabinets so much if they didn't secretly feel just a little guilty. Admitting to sex prejudice, these days, is becoming the same as admitting to racial prejudice—only to be done in secret in sympathetic company. A dissatisfied female employee is an indictment that men who want to consider themselves enlightened don't like to face.

Whats more, in paying for a secretary, a man is paying for ego bolstering. That's why he doesn't hire a man, who would compete with him and go after his job, or a dear old lady who would tend the files like a housewife. He *wants* that subtle deference, that smiling indication that good as she is, she knows he's even better. He's willing to allow a certain amount of ambition and discontent, because that helps to prove that the girl who defers to him wouldn't defer to just any man. It's like a man who's married to a successful woman. It enhances his prestige in a very satisfying way, so long as he doesn't feel personally threatened by it.

Liberationists are not wanted in the office because even the dimmest employer can see that they're going to be trouble. Even if he doesn't mind the scowls, he won't like the lawsuits, union organizing, sitting-in, and sabotage that follow. Girls *do* lose their jobs for these things, and the threat of firing is a deterrent to all but the most committed.

9. I really ought to hire an older woman.
The final, exasperated sigh. He won't of course, at least not until he's old enough and successful enough to have his ego massaged by prestige instead of by girls. Washington is a good town for the older secretary, because power is what excites most of the men there, and in its pursuit the more efficiency the better. And it's a fact that, although there's always an age gap between secretary and boss, it doesn't necessarily widen as the boss gets older. After a point, hiring ever younger secretaries becomes as obvious and laughable as having a series of ever younger wives.

Much has been made, too, of the inability of the older woman to adapt back to the working world after her years away. Why, then, are older secretaries such by-words for loyalty, efficiency and general indispensability? One reason is that it helps to keep them cheap and undemanding if they are made to feel that letting them come to work at all is doing them a favor. All the "concessions" made to them are profits in disguise: a part-time worker, the studies show, produces nearly as much as a full-timer, for half the pay; a housewife "allowed" to work in a bank branch near her home is filling a job that no girl would commute from the center of town to do.

Unmarried girls, these days, are mostly in school or working. Any expansion in the office force must come from married women, and it's coming fast. But it will be a long time before all those who want to work are actually working, so at the moment they are grateful for any job they can get.

As part of the divide-and-rule technique that has always demoralized women workers, the girls who do make their way out of secretaryhood can be used against the ones who stay behind. The unusually intelligent, the very crafty, and those with no other commitments are allowed to rise a few rungs up the ladder. This separates them irrevocably from the rest. The company can then say, "See, you can succeed if you play it *our* way." The women who had hoped that the system would bend a little to accommodate them give up in despair.

It used to be that women could have jobs if they dispensed with having families. Then came the second revolution: they could have both, sometimes even simultaneously. Now there's a third hurdle: can they have *good* jobs and families too?

10. Someone's got to do it.
We're back to women's place as a contingent part of the labor force. A woman supposedly doesn't *need* to work the way a man does, either for the money or the fulfillment. So let her fit in where she's needed.

Is it even true that "someone's got to do it?" Some estimates say that as much as 75 per cent of secretaries' time is wasted The biggest use for many office Xerox machines is copying knitting patterns.

Even so, the work done by the secretary is often more *visible* than that done by her boss. She at least produces a pile of neatly typed papers to be signed at the end of the day; there is often some question about just what he has produced.

The recent spate of executive firings has revealed the white-collar man's insecurity. With no clearly definable, marketable skill, he undergoes a real personality crisis when he finds himself out of work for the first time. Rewriting his résumé to make it sound like something, he wonders what use he is and what he's been doing all these years to justify his large, heavily mortgaged house, his two cars, and the services of his secretary. No wonder he prates about "decision-making," "responsibility," and other managerial mysteries.

He hasn't always and everywhere been accorded the prestige and the money that Western capitalism gives him today.

This emphasis of the business ideology makes a striking comparison with Marxism, in which no value was originally attached to executive competence. For example, Lenin thought that a socialist society could be effectively run with no specially qualified executives.[5]

In fact, if "someone's got to do it" can be applied to his secretary, it is far less clear that it can be applied to him. In some ways, it would make more sense if the value placed on their jobs was reversed.

The ten commonest female comments:

1. *Don't you find it an awfully boring subject?*
2. *Are you a secretary?*
3. *I wish I'd had the opportunities girls have today.*
4. *It's the only job I could get.*
5. *My boss is great.*
6. *We have a lot of fun in my office.*
7. *I'm dying to get married and leave work.*
8. *I couldn't stand to be at home all day.*
9. *It would be nice to work in a small office.*
10. *I'd love to be an airline stewardess.*

The women talking about their office jobs don't mention sex. The innuendoes, jokes, speculations and fantasies that form such a large part of men's views of their secretaries simply don't appear the other way round. To the girls, the office doesn't seem to be a sexy place at all—just a place.

One of the favorite fantasies of the men and the media is that all secretaries want to marry the boss—in fact, that they go to the office in order to husband-hunt. This is not what the girls say. It would be strange if it were, in view of the fact that no more than 5 per cent of office girls in the United States and England actually meet their future mates in the office.

The question of "does she or doesn't she?" so beloved by the popular newspapers, is also greeted with apathy. When asked, the girls report attempted kisses and pinches, but only as annoyances that must be tactfully dealt with. There are some affairs in every office, and they are universally known, although the parties involved invariably think they have kept it secret. The incidence of sex, friendship, love, and passion seem to be about the same as in the "outside world," allowing for the facts that office women are younger than office men (thus it's a question of unmarried girls accepting or rejecting the advances of married men), and that, in most offices, the girls outnumber the men and spend most of their time separated from them.

Without the sexual fantasies that color men's view of the office, it does appear a pretty drab place, and the girls who work there have few illusions about it.

1. Don't you find it an awfully boring subject?
Because they're bored, secretaries think of themselves as boring. This is the saddest and most pervasive thing about their lot. They say, "Oh, I'm just a secretary." They say, "Who would be interested in secretaries? What is there to say about them?"

They have been told so often that their work is secondary and ancillary to the really important things that go on in the company that they have begun to believe it. They have been told so often that it's their own fault they're doing such boring jobs that they have begun to believe that too. The conclusion too many of them have reached is that they must be boring people, unworthy of the attention of writers, liberationists, management trainers, or anyone else.

Secretarial jobs are getting more, not less, boring. One employment agent told me that, while factories are abandoning assembly-line work of the traditional kind on the grounds that its monotony leads to low productivity, offices are attempting to set up factory-like systems of their own. The dictaphone, the computer, the standardized form are taking over where human contact was once the rule.

In addition, secretaries have been losing status. What was once considered a "career" ambition for a clever girl is today scorned by the really ambitious, who see it as domestic slavery transferred to the office. And this kind of scorn, which is often misdirected onto the secretaries themselves, and not onto their jobs, produces a reaction that is self-denigrating and defensive at the same time. Women's liberationists are often astonished at the hostility they get from the women they are "just trying to help," but it shouldn't surprise them, any more than the defensive reaction from the "pieces of meat" on the Miss World reviewing stand.

The secretaries proudest of their jobs are the ones in businesses where there are few women above secretarial rank: the corporations that dominate heavy industry, the more old-fashioned parts of Wall Street, the higher reaches of government. This is true, too, of women in countries where their status is relatively unchanged, like West Germany. There, a college girl almost never becomes a secretary, even at the start of her career. There are few women executives of any kind. And a secretarial job is still, therefore, prized by most women.

The most dissatisfied secretaries are the ones who have seen other women getting nonsecretarial jobs (a fact known to companies, who have refused to promote women on the grounds that it would make the others jealous). They are also the women whose jobs have become more and more routinized, by the introduction of a pool system or by new machinery. They know that what used to seem like a valid career is now becoming mere time-killing.

2. Are you a secretary?
The secretaries' suspicion of the well-meaning interest of outsiders has several sources, only one of which is the criticism they have been subjected to by "liberated" women. Another source is their bosses' suspicion of any disloyalty, a suspicion that is easily aroused by the thought of a secretary talking to someone else about her work. The private ownership of each secretary by her boss (which is a large part of what they both like about the system) makes it almost impossible for secretaries to talk or act like a group, just as it does for wives. Each thinks her own situation is unique, because it is dependent on the personality of one man. For this reason it is hard to imagine secretaries ever forming a union—their status is personal and "confidential," and they see themselves in relation to the boss, not to other secretaries.

There is also the justifiable suspicion that no one outside the system can really understand it, that the secretaries' complaints, satisfactions, loves, and hates only make sense to someone who knows the office world as intimately as they do. This is true to an extent. Blacks have argued that no white can understand their problems, Jews have said the same of Gentiles, and women are currently saying it about men.

But the office world is familiar to almost everyone these days in one way or another, and some of the judgments made from outside have their own kind of validity. "I wouldn't work in an office and turn into a nine-to-five robot" is often heard from students, and although they may eventually be absorbed into the system, perhaps they see some of its drawbacks more clearly before they have their own compromises to defend.

Perhaps the most frequent reason for this question is genuine incredulity that anyone but a secretary is interested in secretaries. The only books aimed at them so far have been manuals and encyclopedias of advice: how to address a letter to an ambassador, what to do when the boss chases you round the desk, how short to wear your skirts. The sexy-secretary stories in newspapers and magazines trivialize or ignore their work, let alone their opinions and ambitions.

Secretaries' anxiety to please has made them an easy group to ignore. A personnel man told me, "Secretaries are the easiest people in the world to motivate." The result was that he could spend all his time thinking about the assembly-line workers, the salesmen, and other more fractious groups.

Because they denigrate their own importance, secretaries do not realize their power. It seems to them that they have little control over the conditions of their work, and until their low expectations change, this will continue to be true.

3. I wish I'd had the opportunities girls have today.
The older generation of working women, particularly those who never married, sometimes wonder what all the fuss is about these days. Don't girls go to college? Don't they get good jobs? Isn't it true that there are more opportunities open to them than they take advantage of? Don't they often voluntarily retreat to the home, undoing all the good work of the pioneers?

This is partly a liberal-conservative argument. Once the worst legal and social barriers are removed, what do you do about people who don't overcome the psychological barriers? Recognize that they're up against real obstacles, or refuse to "coddle" them? Not all the barriers to women's success at work are psychological even today, a fact not always recognized by the "they have every opportunity" school. The fact that progress has been made does not entirely alter the fact that formidable hurdles face the woman trying to get a good job; most of these hurdles will only be finally removed by stiff, enforceable legislation, which is still a long way off.

The women who have "made it" are there to be pointed to, but how much time did they waste on the way just because they were women? How much further would they have gone otherwise? No one can answer this question, because it's impossible to isolate one factor in a career from all the others. But every successful woman has an answer for herself, and it is not always a satisfactory one.

If women aren't as badly off as they might be, or as they once were, that shouldn't be used as an argument for shutting them up now. Alva Myrdal prefaced her feminist book, *Women's Two Roles*,[6] by saying that studying the problems of the underdeveloped world had left her with little heart to tackle the problems of affluent, Western women. This is reasonable, but it doesn't work for those who haven't done anything to help the rest of the world either. Alva Myrdal managed to find time to do both.

But the old-time feminists who see their gains being eroded by the frivolity of others are also talking about the apathy, laziness, and blindness of people who should be among their most ardent supporters. Reformers and revolutionaries have always complained about this. The suffragettes complained about it too. It's a problem in every generation and in every political movement.

Women who use the prejudices of the past (sometimes even exaggerating them) to excuse their own lack of achievement are probably making a step in the right direction. To say, "We just weren't thinking like that then" is less discouraging to a daughter than "Why do you have to do all this? *I* never did." Let them blame it on lack of opportunity if they like—it's largely true, after all, and don't you want your mother to be able to live with herself? This is another instance in which women have to make up their minds whether to blame each other or the system.

4. It's the only job I could get.
This is still much more common than most of the bootstraps
school will admit. Robert Townsend advises the working woman,

> If it's your first job, don't admit you know shorthand or
> typing (although they're good skills to have). You may end
> up in a dead-end secretarial spot. . . .
> If you're passed over because you're a woman, get a job
> with another company.[7]

This advice can come to sound slightly unreal after a job-hunt
that turns up thirty typing tests, ten "We can't hire you without
experience, but if you start as a secretary . . . ," and one "All our
secretaries get a chance at some script-reading too. . . ."

Confused discouragement is the usual response to this experience. Is it her own fault? What has her degree trained her for,
anyway? Maybe they're right. A girl has to know exactly what
she's getting into, and have real confidence in her own talent,
before she has the courage to go on with the hunt or stand up to
the personnel departments who feed her this line.

It's based on the Horatio Alger myth, that anyone who really
wants to make something of himself can do so, and that failure is
always personal. But have enough people made it to verify the
myth? Or, instead, has it been used to stifle legitimate ambitions?

For a secretary trying to sort out this question, one important
thing to remember is that secretarial jobs are only dead-end
because women do them.

> before women were significantly represented on the labour
> market many men started their business careers by doing
> just these jobs . . . . a male secretary would be required to
> act as stand-in and possible successor to the boss. . . . Once
> women enter the labour market the promotional paths be-
> come different. The male clerical jobs become a sort of
> express promotion stream and the jobs available to women
> become what we are all too familiar with, dead-end jobs.[8]

This is a clear indication that if you know what you're doing, you
can use a secretarial job to infiltrate an organization and find out

more about it than you would almost any other way: after all, plenty of men have done just that. It isn't necessarily a waste of time—at first. But you must be ready with a plan to get up or out once you've learned all you can, and that is sometimes harder than starting from scratch in a nonsecretarial job. Most girls find that they have to change companies at this stage in their careers, but every one who has faced this problem has her own solution and a few cautionary tales. The more of them you hear, the better-armed you are likely to be.

5. My boss is great.
The most common consolation girls find for being a secretary is working for a man they respect, admire, and learn from. It can be an extremely valuable stage in a female career, because there are lots of things she can't learn any other way. He has access to the corridors of power, and if she's lucky and he really is a good boss, he will show her how to get there herself.

Too many bosses, interesting though they may be, are too insecure themselves to help their secretaries. They want adulation, not demands. Usually they get more secure the more successful and the older they are, although some of the older generation have antique notions about women that prevent them from being as helpful as they might be.

Proving yourself to one man and then enlisting his help is a method that can't be practiced very widely, and the failure rate is too high for it to be recommended as a genuine solution. But until the real social changes that could affect women's work take place, this is probably the best way to get through the existing jungle.

It can also be a dangerous inducer of complacency. Mere proximity to an able man isn't enough, although many girls are tempted (at first anyway) to think so. Dazzled by his exciting life, it's hard to remember that it isn't *her* life that's exciting. Years later it may strike her with sickening force, only then it's too late to do anything about it.

This system, too, induces the girls who follow it to model themselves on men, a tendency that liberationists deplore. When the girls get their own executive jobs, they're just as aggressive, status-conscious, and mean to their subordinates as the men who made them. But the girls who argue that this shouldn't happen are putting themselves in the position of having to say that there are some "uniquely feminine qualities" (usually things like niceness, sympathy, humility), and that's what they've been attacking men for saying all along. Germaine Greer is more honest when she argues that the "feminine" qualities are, unfortunately, those of the underdog and the eunuch and that as things are now, we may have to choose between being nice and being successful. Everyone will not want to make the same choice; but they should at least realize what the options are.

6. We have a lot of fun in my office.

This is the other great consolation of the office woman. The girl gang provides company, cheer, apartment-sharers, advice, help of all kinds. A girl coming to the big city for her first job would be pretty lost without it. Even after she knows the ropes, it helps her (and everyone else) to get through the day.

It's not true, as is often claimed, that women don't like the company of other women. The only girl in a male company is often accused of liking her status as the only girl, and being even meaner than the men to subsequent female applicants. It can happen, but at least ten times commoner is the girl who refuses (or doesn't go after) a job because "I wouldn't want to be the only woman." It's another double bind: either attitude can be (and has been) used against women workers.

The girl who wants to stay one of the girls is indicating that she knows the pioneer has a rough time, but she is also showing a kind of loyalty that too many successful women forget about. Once they incur the jealousy of the girls they left behind, they are all too likely to scorn the less lucky and the less ruthless and consider themselves the "exceptions" that men tell them they are. If being a woman is what's holding the others back, who wants to be a woman? An understandable attitude, but not a very helpful one.

The girls themselves should beware of hostility to the girl who has been promoted. She has enough problems without their sniping. The company is trying to use divide-and-rule tactics again, and shouldn't be allowed to get away with them. Giving credence to the myth that "women won't work for a woman" can backfire on the spiteful.

Many girls find that life on the lower floors *is* more fun, just the way a kicked-upstairs executive laments his traveling days. The men are younger in the more humble reaches of the company, the atmosphere is livelier and freer from protocol, and the work is often more challenging. The typing pool can be grim, but at its best it can be a lot better than the isolated cubicles attached to each executive's office.

Even at its lowest, the spirit of the typing pool can get the girls through an incredibly boring day, make it bad form to work too hard and show up others, and thus protect the girls from being exploited too much. This leads to complaints from the company, but there really isn't much they can do about it. New girls quickly catch on, and once the atmosphere has become one of resistance, usually because an attempt was made to get too much out of the workers, it's very hard to reverse. This is the famous office "atmosphere" that any temporary typist can gauge a mile off, and that it often takes an outside efficiency expert to change. He will notice things that have long been neglected by the management: timed coffee breaks, lunches in rigid shifts, no mirror in the rest room. His suggestions, which any one of the girls could have made any time she was asked, will be greeted with astonishment.

This atmosphere is also what attracts women back to work from a lonely life of wife-and-motherhood. The office has its drawbacks, but at least she can work sitting down and there's someone to talk to. Offices of returned housewives are often just as giggly as those of seventeen-year-olds—it's almost as if the women had recaptured their youth with their jobs.

7. I'm dying to get married and leave work.
This is the cry that means, "I'm fed up." With no prospects and no money, it's no wonder. Because this is the only work she knows, the office girl attributes her feelings to work itself. The things that oppress her—the routine, the rigid schedule, the rush-

hour traveling, the hurried lunches—can all be relieved by becoming her own mistress, that is, someone's else's wife.

Marriage has two great qualities as a panacea; it gets her out of her parents' or roommates' house and into an establishment of her own, and by freeing her from office work, it gives her the freedom to set her own time schedule. The romance built around the idea of marriage comes later, after the desire to escape is firmly planted.

In fact, much of the romance that used to be associated with marriage has disappeared. No one has escaped the news that not all wives are blissful—the papers are full of divorce, desertion, beatings, and infidelities. The young girl in her first job dreams of adventure, sex, and travel, not of matrimony. But when it comes down to practical alternatives, marriage wins every time. The desire to quit work may antedate the desire for a husband, let alone the desire for a particular man, but for most girls there is no other way out of the frustrations of the office.

Other alternatives seem difficult or impossible. The whole weight of the office girl's culture leads her to look for satisfaction outside work, not within it. The company that hired her as a typist or secretary would have a hard time thinking of her as anything else, even if there were a better job they would give to a woman. She knows too little about other offices to know whether she could get a better deal elsewhere. Her parents, friends, and bosses obviously expect her to get married and leave work—doesn't everybody?

It's a possibility that is open to a woman at just about every stage of her working life, beckoning her to what, on the 8:15 train, can seem like a life of ease and luxury. At the very least, it will assuage her loneliness and give some emotional warmth to her rootless, bewildered life. No one can deny its attractions or say that she should resist them.

8. I couldn't stand to be at home all day.
The other side of the story is usually heard simultaneously. It's a fact that almost all unmarried working girls intend to keep working (or return to work) after marriage and children. It's also

23

a fact that most young wives and mothers, supposedly in the most perfect stage of marital bliss, want to return to work as soon as it's practical. But the reasons are very different for these two groups.

The working girls, fed up though they may be, can't bear the thought of giving up the things they like about their work—the company, the contact with the big world and the men in it, the occasional excitements and breaks in routine. They know that the man they're likely to marry isn't as exciting as the man they might meet tomorrow in the office. They know that the company of small children and other housewives won't be enough to fill their days and their minds satisfactorily. They haven't completely given up the wistful hope that something totally unforeseen might happen to change their lives—and they know it's more likely to happen in New York than in Dubuque.

The woman who goes back to work (or who would like to) has seen some of her worst fears realized. The routine of the household is more numbing than office routine ever was. The loneliness is frightening. Moreover, there's pressure on her—from her husband and everyone else—to do something with herself, to make her life less boring and become a woman other people can still be interested in. Even if she doesn't think typing at the local bank every morning will do the trick, she can't refuse to give it a try. It makes her tireder than ever, but she can't deny that it does her good to get out of the house.

But this remark is most often heard from the complacent girl who's having fun at work, either because she's still young enough to enjoy it or because she's had an unusual success. The contempt of the gay young working girl for the housewife may be unattractive, but at least it's short-lived: she'll get caught too, and although she won't remember the things she used to say about "those frumps," her perspective will change completely.

9. *It would be nice to work in a small office.*
The girl who's getting bored, but isn't ready to throw in the towel yet, usually envisions heaven as a different kind of office—smaller, bigger, younger, older, or in a different field. The grass is greener for everyone. Girls in show biz complain it's too ruthless,

girls in law offices complain it's too drab; either there's too much pressure or too little. But there are some enduring myths about what kind of office is attractive.

A small office is favored because there's usually more variety. Where there's one girl instead of fifty, she can do the phone, the letters, everything. She also has exclusive access to the men, who never notice one particular girl among the dozens in a large pool. She is valued and can indeed make herself indispensable. Some leeway is given to her in setting her own methods and schedule.

Many girls dream of making their way up the social scale by changing offices. One told me, "I'd love to work for a Harley Street man." Chic new offices are overrated as a draw; atmosphere is much more important, but seems to be best in young, new companies that haven't had time to build up too much protocol. So a lively atmosphere often goes with fashionable surroundings.

Real as these distinctions are, the truth is that the office girl doesn't see her job as changing very much. She knows she'll just be doing more or less the same thing in a different place. Change itself becomes a substitute for progress, and some girls are always job-hunting as a last-ditch way to stave off the feeling of being trapped. This is why their terms of reference are often things like the size, location, and appearance of the office—not the work that goes on inside. It's not the secretary's concern how much the company makes or how it fares; her portion will be the same whatever happens. She is just an invisible cog in the giant wheel.

10. I'd love to be an airline stewardess.

This is the classic escape line, and the classic female ambition in our society. Such a career seems to have done away with the "work" part of work, leaving only the fun fringes: travel, men, and charm. Two stewardesses who wrote a book about their experiences sum up the appeal the job has for so many girls:

> It was my chance to escape, as Carolyn Jones did, and Cyd Charisse, to become big movie stars. I wasn't reaching for

> stardom, as they did. I just wanted to swing a little more
> than I was destined to in Amarillo. . . .
>
> Rachel grew up in Louisville very much as I did in a happy
> family with lots of friends and all the usual high school fun.
> By the time she was a senior she was getting restless. She
> didn't want to stay a small town girl with a small town job.
> She'd looked over all the local boys and found none exciting
> enough to give her the life she wanted.[9]

It used to be that going to the big city to become a secretary
fulfilled this kind of ambition. Often, it still does. But office life is
now too much the common lot of women to have the charm of
novelty or excitement. Unless it involves travel or glamor, it
isn't enough. Waitressing on airplanes, too, is losing some of its
appeal as air travel becomes more commonplace.

The desire to escape work altogether, because it is a world that
has severely disappointed women, is at the back of many of these
ambitions. To the girls who want fun and freedom, these things
seem still to be rewards dished out to women by men in the form
of attention, admiration, dates, and, finally, support. The liberationists seem to such girls to be killjoys and humorless school-
marms.

But how far will women be able to run? How many of them
will never get that trip around the world, that date with a movie
star? And how many more will find that even the fulfilling of such
dreams doesn't really solve the problem of what to do with their
lives? Eventually they will have to make some attempt to widen
the desperate set of alternatives they are offered now.

Chapter Two
THE RISE OF THE SECRETARY

IN THE GREAT debate about working women, it is often forgotten that women have always worked. Only very recently has the work of more than a tiny minority of them been confined to the care of a husband, two or three children, and a small house filled with conveniences. Alice Rossi observes, "for the first time in the history of any known society, motherhood has become a full-time occupation for adult women."[1]

The plight of the modern housewife *without* children is even more historically bizarre. She is cut off from the productive work of her society in a way that no other woman has ever been.

> It is often assumed that the woman worker was produced by the Industrial Revolution, and that since that time women have taken an increasing share in the world's work. This theory is, however, quite unsupported by facts. In every industiral system in the past women have been engaged in productive work and their contribution has been recognized as an indispensable factor.[2]

The idleness and uselessness of the "clinging vine" Victorian ideal woman provided some of the impetus behind the women's rights movement at the end of the last century. Similarly, the bored housewives identified by Betty Friedan, clamoring to go back to work, are changing today's accepted ideas about women. But these women are, and always have been, a statistical minority, and the pretense that all women are "ladies," who can choose to be kept in idleness if they wish, has been used to weaken seriously the position of all working women.

A use of intimidation in one class and envy in another effectively prevents solidarity. The young middle-class woman could be frightened into social and sexual conformity with the specters of governessing, factory work, or prostitution. And the less favored female is left only to dream of becoming a lady, the single improvement of her situation she is permitted to conceive of, the hope of acquiring social and economic status through attracting the sexual patronization of the male.[3]

The myth that work outside the home is not really suitable for women, and that it is only justified by unusually hard times or family misfortune, has been used to keep women's work at the level of the lowest drudgery. Any improvement in her lot might tempt her to stay there and enjoy it, with who knows what consequences for the home?

It has often been pointed out how strange it is that this set of myths should coexist with tolerance of the most desperate and degrading work conditions for women, and with propaganda *for* female employment when the economy demands it. In nineteenth-century America,

Public moralists...acclaimed the factory employment of women. In these men's views women who did not respond to the call would be "doomed to idleness and its inseparable attendants, vice and guilt..." Woman's place was thus not in the home, according to our founders, but wherever her "more important" work was.[4]

The pressure for removal of the barriers to female employment coexisted with pressure for protective legislation for the exploited female factory worker. The confusion between these two movements, and between the two sorts of women involved in them, is the source of many of the confusions about women's work today. Do women want to work, or is work an unfortunate necessity from which they want to escape to the shelter of the home? Is it an added burden, or a privilege? "Women" and "work" are treated in such questions as if they were all the same, and as if a generalization could be made.

But this is absurd. One might as well argue that because a factory worker agitates for a shorter working day he should envy the lot of an unemployed miner; or that the example of a lawyer complaining about his tax bill could be used to deter a longshoreman from striking for higher pay.

Today, there are women struggling to escape the confines of their secretarial jobs. There are also women aspiring hopefully to just such jobs. The one group is not ungrateful nor the other misguided. They are simply in different situations. And one way of unraveling the confusion between them is to look at how both these situations came about.

The Industrial Revolution did not create the woman worker. It merely removed most productive work from the home, so that anyone who wanted to do such work had to follow it to factory, mill, and (eventually) office. Child care could not be combined with other tasks in the old way, nor could the few remaining household jobs: cleaning, laundry, meal preparation. The housewife had fewer jobs than before, but the ones she had were still done in the old, inefficient way.

For a woman to stay at home, to look after the children and the house, she could only do such paid work as could be done at home. This included piecework from factories, taking in lodgers, sewing, and laundry. All were lamentably low-paid. In order to take a more lucrative job outside the home, a woman had either to neglect her children or pay for them to be minded elsewhere. Generally, it was cheaper for the economy to keep young mothers at home than to arrange things so that they could go out to work, by providing crèches and nursery schools.

So the myth grew up that all women were mothers, that this dilemma affected them all, and that therefore the ideal was for them to stay at home. Reinforcing this was the picture of the "lady," whose leisure and culture reflected favorably on the man who supported her. The house-bound woman had less and less idea of what went on in the "real" world outside her four walls, and her useful functions were supplanted by futile socializing and decorative crafts. She began to give substance to the notion that she was "unsuited" to work.

Working-class women continued to follow their work out of the home. Their health and their children suffered because they did so, and thus they provided horrendous examples of the "evils of women's work" for the moralists to point to, but they had no alternative.

As for the middle-class women who were *not* supported by men, there was no place at all for them in the scheme of things. Neither inured to the rigors of working life nor financially able to keep up their genteel pretensions, they starved in miserable silence.

The world of men's work was changing during this era too. With the spread of industrialization, their work was moving outside the home. The weaver and the smith went to the factory. Artisans of every kind were turned into machine operators. And to supervise the whole operation, the middle-class man became a manager and hired a clerk.

The old professions had required only a study or a consulting room. The management of property could be done with a simple ledger. There was no particular reason to separate the office from the home. If the business were large enough to require employees, they could be recruited from among the dispossessed and the younger sons of the literate classes, who had no property of their own. Such a group had existed for centuries, and during the Middle Ages it was largely absorbed by the church. The word *clerk* has the same root as *cleric*.

> When, during the fifteenth and sixteenth centuries, [the clerk's] association with holy orders became more tenuous, he acquired a number of new techniques, including that of double-entry bookkeeping, and subsequently attained a tolerable status and a fair degree of security, if not affluence, as a servant of the rising merchant class. This position he maintained until the middle of the nineteenth century; in the last hundred years, however, the extension of education, the development of office machinery, and the infiltration

into the clerical field of large numbers of women, have brought about radical changes in his functions and status.[5]

As industrial production and commerce increased, management became more complex. Clerks were needed in ever larger numbers to keep the accounts and answer the correspondence. At this point the office came into being. Here, for the first time, was a wholly middle-class work place. There was no danger of having to rub shoulders with the sweaty workers or to endure the noise and dust of heavy machinery. The clerks who worked in the new office generally identified themselves with the managers, although few rose to this position themselves. Either they were the sons of owners, being trained to take over the business, or they were simply employees. The existence of the former, who often worked just for the experience, severely depressd the wages of the latter, who had trouble keeping up the middle-class appearance expected of them. Their wives often did factory piecework, being too busy at home or too genteel to venture out to the factory itself.

In Dickens's day, the office was small, dismal, and all-male. The shipping office in *Dombey and Son*, written about 1846–48, is typical of the breed.

Such vapid and flat daylight as filtered through the ground-glass windows and skylights, leaving a black sediment upon the panes, showed the books and papers, with the figures bending over them, enveloped in a studious gloom, and as much abstracted in appearance, from the world without, as if they were assembled at the bottom of the sea; while a mouldy little strong-room in the obscure perspective, where a shady lamp was always burning, might have represented the cavern of some ocean-monster, looking on with a red eye at these mysteries of the deep.

When Perch the messenger, whose place was on a little bracket, like a timepiece, saw Mr. Dombey come in ... he hurried into Mr. Dombey's room, stirred the fire, quarried fresh coals from the bowels of the coal box, hung the newspaper to air upon the fender, put the chair ready, and the screen in its place, and was round upon his heel on the instant of Mr. Dombey's entrance to take his great coat and hat, and hang them up. . . .

Between Mr. Dombey and the common world, as it was accessible through the medium of the outer office—to which Mr. Dombey's presence in his own room may be said to have struck like damp, or cold air—there were two degrees of descent. Mr. Carker in his own office was the first step; Mr. Morfin, in *his* own office, was the second. Each of these gentlemen occupied a little chamber like a bath-room, opening from the passage outside Mr. Dombey's door. . . .

"How do you do this morning?" said Mr. Carker the manager, entering Mr. Dombey's room soon after his arrival one day, with a bundle of papers in his hand.

"How do you do, Carker?" said Mr. Dombey, rising from his chair, and standing with his back to the fire. "Have you anything there for me?"

"I don't know that I need trouble you, returned Carker, turning over the papers in his hand. "You have a committee today at three, you know."[6]

This passage shows very clearly the relationships of the various office workers of the time. It is interesting to see how the functions of today's secretary are divided among the messenger or officeboy, the manager, and the clerk. Personal services and office functions are divided up, but the amount of delegation seems to be about the same as in today's boss-secretary arrangement. The difference is that these days, Mr. Dombey would be unlikely to be the owner of the business; he would be the manager, and Mr. (or Miss) Carker would be his secretary.

This environment, cramped, private, and obsequious, nonetheless represented a haven for the unsupported middle-class woman. Then, as now, it was not really the bored, affluent wife who demanded access to the office. It was the woman who more or less had to work, and who simply wanted an employment more suited to her status than factory work or domestic service. There were several reasons why the office seemed the answer to her prayers.

One was the depressed state of the traditional "genteel" feminine occupations. The oversupply of governesses made it desperately hard to get such jobs, and the low pay meant that the distinction between the governess and the household servants was continually eroded. Uniform, or at least drab clothing, was required, and of course the girl had to live with the family whose children she taught. Resented by the servants and treated with contempt by the family, her life was lonely and narrow.

Work at home, such as dressmaking, brought in nowhere near enough to live on. As Charles Booth, in his study of *London Labour and the London Poor,* found, "It is notorious that the middle class needlewoman is paid less than any decent factory girl in the East End."

In the United States, a girl could teach in the rapidly expanding school system, but conditions for teachers were far worse than for many factory workers. The mill girls of Lowell, Massachusetts, for instance, prized their jobs and the well-equipped dormitories that went with them. Teachers, on the other hand, boarded with local families, and their morals and manners were strictly scrutinized. They were hired because they could be paid less than half as much as men; even at double the women's wages, only the most desperate men would consent to take teaching jobs.

Nursing had also been opened to women, but here too, dedication, poverty, and appalling conditions were the rule. Office work offered, for the first time, the hope of an occupation that did not involve "living in."

The traditional Victorian family no longer provided much of a haven for its spinsters. The aunts and cousins and unmarried daughters who had proved so useful when a household did its own sewing, baking, churning, and preserving were nothing but a drain on the resources of the citified family, and they were often bullied and exploited. In fact, their status went a long way to explode the myth of the woman "kept in idleness." So-called idle wives at least bore children, even when they did not rear them. In the upper strata, they served a social function as well. But the woman with no economic function at all, who was a liability in a money economy, was scarcely pampered; spinsters had to find an occupation.

To make matters worse, their numbers were growing. The men of America were moving westwards, and although many of them settled farms, for which they needed the help of wives and children, many went as trappers, traders, prospectors, and soldiers. The West was a male preserve, and the consequence was that the East was full of spinsters. The Civil War did away with another three million men.

The situation in England was no better:

Emigration to America and the developing Empire ... deprived this country ... of thousands of young men of marriageable age. About 5 million young people, mostly men, left Britain between 1830 and 1875. "The excess of the emigration of males over. females," reports the Registrar General, "accounts for the present difference in the proportion of the sexes." In spite of efforts by the British Ladies' Female Emigrant Society and the Female Middle Class Emigration Society, "few women above the servant class emigrated."[7]

Even the women who did manage to catch a man were afflicted by a new sense of their own expendability. Wives saw their own status diminishing as their productive work grew less, and the women's rights movement was by no means confined to spinsters alone.

The restlessness and sense of futility among middle-class women of the Victorian era ... was the subjective counterpart of the economic and social changes wrought by the Industrial Revolution. The "clinging vine" ideal, in fashion then, was the unconscious expression of a social situation in which women had lost their economic usefulness and had to rely exclusively on their "charms" to catch a husband, and on public morality to retain him.[8]

Office work was obviously suited to the limited talents of the "clinging vine"—it was sedentary, detailed, monotonous, and indoors. It did involve unchaperoned contact with men, but at least the men were likely to be of the woman's own class.

The opening of the office to women was accompanied by a great deal of cant about giving impoverished ladies the chance to earn an honest living. When they were admitted to the British Post Office, in 1872, the Postmaster General examined each applicant himself to make sure that he selected only really deserving cases. Although the post office saved a great deal of money by hiring women, and its critics said that this was the only reason for the new policy, work was spoken of as almost a form of charity.

The compelling reason for this expansion of the labor force was that office work was outstripping the supply of people who could do it.

> The demand for clerical workers has grown so rapidly that it could not have been met if employers had insisted on hiring only men. Most clerical work requires an education well above the average that prevailed at the end of the last century. The supply of young people who were qualified and available for clerical employment included many more girls than young men. More girls than boys attended and graduated from school but ... fewer went on to college.[9]

All over the industrialized world, imperial expansion meant more trade and thus more paperwork. Machine production required more sophisticated knowledge of market forces, distribution, and production techniques. The modern communications network was being established, and government regulation of all these activities was necessary for the first time.

Just as factory work was considered "suitable" for women when they were needed to do it, and teaching became "suitable" when it suffered a labor shortage, it was now discovered that women's dexterity, patience, and docility made them ideal for the office. To disarm male suspicion of their new competitors, careful distinctions were made at first between women's and men's work.

In fact, women did not generally take over jobs previously held by men; the whole structure of office work was adjusted to give them only the routine and subservient functions. Thus, their advent could be explained to the men as freeing them for higher things.

> As in manufacturing, new jobs were created, which from the beginning were allocated to women. Most of the new jobs involved less skill, knowledge, responsibility, prestige, and pay than the old clerical occupations.... The old meanings of the terms "clerk" and "secretary" are preserved today only in such special titles as "County Clerk" and "Secretary and Treasurer."[10]

New technology helped women get to the office, because it provided whole new categories of work that no one, man or woman, had ever done, and thus the question of usurpation did not arise. The new machines with the biggest impact were the telephone and the typewriter, both of which are still practically female monopolies.

The typewriter was introduced to the public in 1873, and Remington had the revolutionary idea of training girls to demonstrate it. Called "typewriters" themselves, the girls created a sensation, and the firms that bought the machines wanted the operators too. Typing was seized on by women as a golden opportunity to get out to work, and men said, "Of course—they can play the piano, so it's not surprising that they can type."

The first typewriting course offered by a New York business school attracted two hundred applicants for ten openings, and typewriting was soon being taught in commercial colleges and public high schools, as well as by the typewriter companies themselves.

Britain was slower to adopt the typewriter. Predictably, the new machine made its first mark in the fast-growing government bureaucracy.

> When the telegraph system was nationalised in 1870, the Post Office brought in about a dozen women. Twenty years

later, with the introduction of typewriters, Whitehall found
to its alarm that women typists were necessary. But they
were carefully locked into their top floor offices, while the
one woman in the Board of Agriculture was tucked safely
away in a small and dingy basement.[11]

The telegraph provided, as we have seen, some of the first opportunities for office women. The telephone opened up many
more. Founded in the United States in 1876, the Bell system
quickly became a female preserve. By 1902 there were 37,000
women operators and only 2,500 men. In England, young boys
(who earned about as much as women) were tried first, but they
were restless and impatient. Women were quickly substituted.
Women were admitted first to the areas that were growing
fastest, and also to those that were least attractive to men. The
public communications network offered fewer opportunities for
money-making than did private business, and the civil service was
not the first hope of the budding entrepreneur. Thus, these were
the jobs opened to women.

By the turn of the century women were firmly entrenched in
certain types of clerical work. In telephonic and telegraphic
offices they formed 45% of all employees; in local government 29%, and in the civil service 25%. In commerce they
were still a small minority, and in banking, insurance and
law there was strong resistance to their employment.[12]

Even these limited concessions, however, unleashed a deluge
unforeseen by any of the first employers of office women. By
1890, women held 15 per cent of the clerical jobs in the United
States. Ten years later, one third of all office workers were female.
The girls who were admitted to American high schools so that
they could become teachers were well-prepared for the office.
Elementary education for both sexes became compulsory in
England in 1870, and secondary education followed in 1902.
Education has always been the distinguishing mark of the
clerk, and the comparative scarcity of literate employees gave
him his prestige. This advantage was now being eroded. The

demand for clerks was one impetus behind the growth of the educational system, but the influence of universal education on the status of the office worker was profoundly destructive.

With the drop in the prestige of clerical work, some of its traditional disadvantages were more keenly felt. Clerks had always been under attack from above and below—scorned by their employers for their pretensions to gentility, they were also despised and resented by workingmen because although they too were employees, they pretended to be a cut above the actual laborer. They were the carriers of messages from the boss, his representatives and mouthpieces, although their status did not bring them much of a reward. Indeed, the standards a clerk had to keep up—black coat, white collar, good school for his sons— often made him struggle harder to make ends meet than did the worker.

There was something pathetic about the clerk, who could neither bargain like a wage-worker nor live like a boss. It became desperately important to him to keep up his pretensions, which were often all he had in the world.

> One of the dominating features of the clerical conscious-ness at this time was the conception of the "gentleman." The ideal of the gentleman in the second half of the nineteenth century, being essentially defined as a state of mind and a corresponding mode of conduct, was an inexpensive luxury. Gentlemanliness was still within the reach of those clerks whose salaries would not support a proper middle-class style of life. It was also sufficiently vague as a value that gentle-manliness and respectability could become curiously con-fused in the lower-middle-class culture in which clerks played a major role....
>
> Frankness and forthrightness are functions of economic independence; unpretentiousness is a function of social inde-pendence. In both respects, the clerk generally lacked the necessary security. The conditions of his work and the orientations of his life very often brought the opposite qualities of obsequiousness, circumlocution and pretentiousness to the fore.... His distinguishing mark was respectability.[13]

The clerk's bid for respectability rested on his contact with the bosses and his emulation of their ways. He adopted many of the conservative attitudes that one would expect to find in the property-owning classes, but which have often seemed incongruous in employees. This paradoxical state of affairs is true of the office to this day.

The clerk's self-esteem also rested on his accomplishments: literacy, bookkeeping, shorthand. But these things, as the clerk quickly found out, had no absolute value in themselves—their value was determined by the market.

Shorthand, for instance, enjoyed a tremendous vogue throughout the nineteenth century. Rival systems were invented and advertised, contests were held, and it was considered as enjoyable and absorbing a pastime as crossword puzzles are today. Its practical use began with the taking down of sermons for publication, and quickly extended to the law courts and the newspapers, and through them to the office in general. As late as 1888, a book called *How to Succeed as a Stenographer or Typewriter* is addressed mainly to men: "There are comparatively few verbatim reporters, and the young shorthand writer who has reached that distinction should consider that it gives him the rank of a scholar and a gentleman."[14]

But such inflated claims were already being exploded. A year earlier, an International Shorthand Congress was held in London, at which, ominously enough, there was even an address on "Shorthand for Women."

> The conference of 1887 was the dying splutter of the candle. ... It was the last great onslaught of shorthand on the popular imagination ... changing ideas led to shorthand enthusiasts being regarded as cranks; the advent of more and more girls into offices as stenographers eventually brought shorthand into the line of "something for the girls," and from that it has gradually emerged as a subject which is dealt with in the office from nine till five, and is then forgotten.[15]

The introduction of women to the office was the final blow to the clerk's self-esteem. At first, their typing and telephoning did not interfere with his bookkeeping and correspondence, but the obvious advantages of combining shorthand with typing meant that soon the girls were learning both. Before long, there was very little in the clerk's job that could not be done by a woman.

> The work which already carried the stigma of being "unmasculine" was one of the first middle-class occupations to become a feminine preserve of employment. "Born a man, died a clerk" took on an added social significance as a result. The influx of women merely strengthened the popular stereotype of the clerk and further detracted from the prestige of the occupation.
>
> The effect of a high proportion of women in an occupation on the social status of that occupation is a function of the general status of women in society. And here the relationships of sexual inequality within the family have been duplicated in the relationships of sexual inequality in the occupational world.[16]

Even more important was the fact that, like women teachers, women clerks would work for very much less than men.

> These women came either without any previous experience of business, or from occupations in which the earnings were very poor by comparison with the average pay of a clerk. They were offered and willingly accepted lower wages than would have been proposed to men for the work; and before many years had passed they (or other women) were to be found doing general clerical work, often for less money than the shorthand-typist could command.[17]

At first, the new competition and the consequent depression of salaries shook the clerks out of their political conservatism. Much has been made of this class's hostility to unions and to left-wing ideas in general, but it is also true that many of the radicals at the turn of the century came from the lower middle class. The man whose livelihood was provided by the new industrial and imperial technology was not likely to be committed to the older business methods favored by the traditional property owner. Writers from the owner class, like Morris and Ruskin, saw the machine as ruining the pastoral beauty of England and its harmoniously feudal social system. But

> Wells, along with Kipling, is part of a more general movement in the later nineteenth century that sought to bring literature into contact with the new life shaped by the steamship and the airplane and lived by technicians and scientists, as well as poets.[18]

Both these writers were office employees as, later, were many of the Fabian socialists. Sidney Webb was president of the Association of Shorthand Writers and Typists, founded in 1903. Bernard Shaw, whose interest in simplified orthography was one of the last manifestations of the shorthand craze, described himself as follows:

> I have worked in an office. . . . The class in which I was born was that most unlucky of all classes: the class that claims gentility and is expected to keep up its appearances without more than the barest scrap and remnant of property to do it on.[19]

The young radical, serving time in an office and ardently reading the works of social reformers, is a familiar figure in the novels of the time.

With socialism went an interest in women's rights, which offset to some extent the jealousy aroused by competition for jobs. The earliest office-workers' unions included both men and women, although women's growing monopoly of office work soon led to separate unions. By 1911, in England,

> the Association had outgrown its nervousness about "trade union" associations and practices, but had also taken on a more definitely "feminist" mentality . . . men (who had been a small and diminishing factor) were excluded altogether, and the title became "The Association of Women Clerks and Secretaries."[20]

The sexes had separate unions until 1939.

What averted large-scale industrial action among white-collar workers was not lack of feeling on their part, but simply the rapid expansion of opportunities. Clerical wages dropped; but it is misleading to take this as the only index of how men fared in the office. The men who were still on the lower levels suffered severely from female competition; but more and more of them moved into jobs that would now be called managerial. Clerks who were able to specialize did so. Many formed quasi-professions out of their specialties and became accountants, company secretaries, efficiency experts, and personnel managers. Companies grew and split into divisions, each with its body of expertise—marketing, product development, production.

Many of these groups of experts have managed to institute training requirements and professional associations. This limits access to their jobs, and therefore, in effect, limits the jobs to men. This has become the most successful way of combating the tide of female competition, and it is still going on—such groups have become progressively more "technical" in their training and methods, and they are now joining the trend to white-collar unionism. The gulf between them and the "generalists," mainly women, is still growing.

With the decline of the owner-manager, these men have moved into positions of greater power than many of them would ever have known under the old paternalist system. It is no longer ludicrous for them to identify with the bosses; they *are* the bosses. Corporate management, payment in stock options, and absentee boards of directors have all helped to blur the line between ownership and management, until in some companies it can scarcely be said to exist at all.

So the conservative atmosphere of the office has remained fairly unchanged, although now Mr. Carker is in Mr. Dombey's shoes, and it is Mr. Carker's female secretary who fools herself into believing that the boss's interests are identical with her own.

The routinization of office jobs as they were taken over by women meant that the women were not in exactly the same situation as the men they replaced. In many ways, the female secretary, once she learned shorthand and gained access to the inner sanctum, did what the clerk used to do—she took down replies to letters, kept the appointment book, received visitors— but she did not normally act on her own in business matters. The erstwhile clerk, now promoted to office manager, kept the junior typist, the office-boy, and the salesmen in line. He was empowered to do business on behalf of the boss. He kept the accounts. The secretary sometimes took over some of these functions too, but only if they did not involve policy decisions. Power of any real kind was kept firmly out of her hands.

The traditional male clerk had been valuable largely because of his expertise in a particular firm, and this continued to be true. For instance, Leonard Bast, the clerk in E. M. Forster's *Howard's End,* loses his job through the well-meaning inter- ference of the genteel heroines. He explains that he knew how to do one job in one particular company; now that he has lost that, he's no use to anyone.

A girl's work, because it was routine and mechanical, was from the first entirely transferable. There was a scale of expertise from the simple typist through the shorthand-typist to the personal secretary, but the tasks were the same in every office. This meant that almost every literate girl could do the work. The same middle-class families that had provided most of the male clerks now sent their daughters to work in the office. A woman writing in 1902 observes,

> Some curious results of the movement in favour of securing economic independence for women may be observed at the present time. The theory has of course in many cases been reduced in its application to an absurdity. Parents who thirty years ago would have expected all their daughters to stay at home until they were married, now with equal un- wisdom wish them to pass from the school to the office, regardless of their natural bent, and as careless of their future prospects as before.[21]

Once fathers found out that their daughters could contribute to the family income without losing caste, they were all in favor of sending them out to work. Those with some residual prejudice in the matter still allowed typing by the sheet at home, which brought in enough to dress the girl, if not to offset entirely the cost of her keep.

Even the girls who went out to the office still lived at home, giving rise to the "they only work for pin-money" theory that has plagued women workers to this day. As Booth pointed out,

> The middle class parent imagines that he is doing his daughter a kindness when he pays the cost of her board and lodging for her, and lets her work ten and a half hours a day for what she is proud to call "only pocket money." He is in fact making a present to his daughter's employer.[22]

This system was particularly hard on those girls who *did* have to make their own living, and whose situation was scarcely better than that of women in the older occupations.

> The conditions and cost of living of women clerks vary in many and important respects from those of women teachers. Their work is less exhausting on the whole and less trying to the nerves. But, on the other hand, their holidays are generally very short; except for a few brief months in the year, they must work while it is day, and seek for their amusements when night comes; they are doing sedentary work in office hours, and yet only by a strong determination can they find any recreation except in the further sedentary occupations of reading and sewing, or in poisonous lecture halls, concert rooms, or theatres. They cannot easily do their shopping, and have no opportunity of wearing out their shabby dresses in private; they must feed themselves unwholesomely at tea-rooms, or extravagantly and monotonously at restaurants. Above all, whereas teaching may be regarded as a life work well worth doing for its own sake, clerical work can hardly be soul-satisfying to any intelligent human being. It is not living, but merely a means of living.[23]

What a familiar picture this is to today's secretary, shopping during her lunch-hour and living on sandwiches and yogurt!

The fear of contact with strange men, which was felt both by the women themselves and by their parents and employers on their behalf, narrowed the scope of their lives even further than necessary. In the post office, "ladies" were not allowed to serve the public: such jobs were reserved for men or for working-class women. In all offices, the first women were incarcerated. The Post Office Savings Bank in London, which employed 130 women, was typically reassuring: "A private staircase leads up to this part of the building, and a dining-room and kitchen are attached to it, in order that no communication need be carried on with the other floors."[24]

The women were not allowed out of the building at all during the day, and money for the company-provided meals was deducted from their pay.

Another fear that haunted the pioneers was that in order to get the new jobs, women had to live in the cities that contained them, and this often meant that women had to live on their own. Previously, women's occupations had involved living arrangements as well, and indeed the office women's salaries made it difficult for them to manage respectably on their own.

One early and successful solution was the establishment of hostels and hotels, run by charitable organizations. The Y.W.C.A. was started to fill the need of working girls for cheap, respectable quarters, and the W.C.T.U., the churches, and some private people started other such schemes.

The drawbacks were obvious: the women in the hostels had little privacy and even less freedom; they were locked in at an appointed hour, smoking and drinking were often banned, and male callers were confined to the public rooms. On the other hand, such places were the saving of many an impoverished, newly arrived typist who knew no one in the big city and had scarcely been out of her parents' drawing room before.

By the turn of the century, the typewriting market was almost as glutted as the governess market had been. Ladies blamed the situation on the mistaken policy of educating the daughters of the working class, who then competed with them for jobs. The daughters of the professional classes, who were still barred from entering the professions, found themselves in exactly the same job market as the working-class girls looking for an alternative to domestic service. The lumping together of all female office workers began to engender the hostility and factionalism that have continued to this day.

In 1889, about half the working women in Britain were domestic servants. At the turn of the century, the proportion was dropping towards one third. It was about the same in the United States, where 40 per cent of employed women were domestics in 1900. One English lady remarked to the *British Weekly* investigators: "I hope before long we shall see the work done by machinery, for in London young women will even go into the Salvation Army sooner than become servants." The office, of course, was an even more attractive alternative.

The First World War took the pressure off the job market, and provided office work for both servant girl and bourgeoise girl. It has been estimated that in the United Kingdom alone, 200,000 women went into offices during the war, and many of them stayed. "Between 1911 and 1921 the number of male clerks increased a little more slowly than the occupied population while the number of female clerks increased more than three times."[25]

It is in this period that the independent working girl becomes a recognized female type, and not just a spinster eking out her pathetic existence or a daughter waiting for marriage. She has become interesting because she is the first woman in at least a hundred years to have a measure of independence; her life can contain the unexpected. Although the city was full of traps and perils for the naïve office girl, her education in the ways of the world, her struggle to keep up standards, and (in popular writing at least) the triumph of her virtue over all temptations made a lively and dramatic tale. As C. Wright Mills points out, "Ten years on either side of the First World War—that was the time of the greatest literary interest in the white-collar girl.[26]

J. B. Priestley's *Angel Pavement* provides a fine specimen of the type, Miss Matfield. The daughter of an impoverished country doctor, she works in a small London office, lives in a residence club, and isn't getting any younger. Her status at work is still in some doubt—one of her employers says, when discussing possible economics, "'Get rid of the girl, right away, without 'esitation. They never should have started girls in the City. The place has never been right since. Powderin' noses! Cups o' tea! You don't know where y'are.'"[27] When the business flourishes, however, a second female typist is added to the staff, one of the "third class."

> The girls who earn their keep by going to offices and working typewriters may be divided into three classes. There are those who, like Miss Matfield, are the daughters of professional gentlemen and so condescend to the office and the typewriter, who work beneath them just as girls once married beneath them. There are those who take it all simply and calmly, because they are in the office tradition, as Mr. Smeeth's (the chief clerk's) daughter would have been. Then there are those who rise to the office and the typewriter, who may not make any more money than their sisters and cousins who work in factories and cheap shops—they may easily make considerably less money—but nevertheless are able to cut superior and ladylike figures in their respective family circles because they have succeeded in becoming typists.[28]

Women's office jobs are apportioned on the basis of this class structure, and the implication is that there is not much movement from one category to another. A junior typist remains one until she marries; a shorthand-typist or secretary stays one until *she* marries, which is a more unlikely prospect—she has been driven to the office in the first place by the lack of marriage material.

Miss Matfield's job holds out no particular prospects; like the two male clerks in the office, she is only hoping that the company will keep going and that she won't suddenly find herself out of work in an increasingly crowded market. But she knows that only marriage will significantly change her financial situation, and the question is whether she will be able to hold out for someone suitable, instead of simply grabbing the first offer.

Her residence club, the Burpenfield, is respectable but institutional, and it represents for her all the dreary horrors of her life if she fails to marry.

> What Miss Matfield . . . disliked most about the Burpenfield was the presence of all the other members, whose life she had to share. There were too many of them, and their mode of life was like an awful parody of her own. The thought that her own existence would seem to an outsider just like theirs infuriated or saddened her, for she felt that really she was quite different from these others, much superior, a more vital, splendid being. . . . Then there were the women older than herself, downright spinsters in their thirties and early forties, who had grown gray and withered at the typewriter and the telephones, who knitted, droned on interminably about dull holidays they had had, took to fancy religions, quietly went mad, whose lives narrowed down to a point at which washing stockings became the supreme interest. . . . Sometimes, when she was tired and nothing much was happening, Miss Matfield saw in one of these women an awful glimpse of her own future, and then she rushed into her bedroom and made the most fantastic and desperate plans, not one of which she ever attempted to carry out.[29]

Towards the end of the book she dreams of becoming a real businesswoman, but it is obviously just a dream. She doesn't know how to go about it and sees it as a consolation prize—another way of achieving the standard of living that should have come with marriage, but not an end in itself.

The swelling of the female office population has not yet begun to push women up the career ladder, which still seems a very poor second to marriage. But it has made possible a stratification of the women in the office, reflecting the class structure of the society that has produced them. Within this structure, an office type is beginning to emerge. She is single, in her twenties, with a high-school education. She is more likely, in America, to be native born than is typical of the population at large.

One of the first real sociological studies of the American office girl was carried out in Minneapolis in 1925. Taking a sample of 8,200 clerical workers, 58 per cent of whom were female, the study concluded, "There is a very general preference for single women in clerical work."[30] Employers indicated that there was an age ladder in their offices as well as a status ladder: age 20–25 produced the best typists, 25–30 the best stenographers, and over 30 the best bookkeepers. Half the women sampled were between 18 and 25. When asked what educational level they looked for, 64 per cent of the bosses said high school. More (8 per cent) said "none" than said college or university (7 per cent). "The general attitude of the employers was that they did not feel that general education was of any value to their employees." The limitation of clerical jobs that had begun to bother girls like Miss Matfield was already being built into the system. Many of the bosses felt that hiring college-educated girls was simply asking for trouble; and the majority of the employees studied had high-school diplomas and no further training.

Partly, this reflects the American emphasis on the self-made businessman or woman. The heroine of Sinclair Lewis's novel *The Job*, published in 1916, is forced into the office by the death of her father. She enters a world of crude competition, and from a shy typist becomes a sharp real-estate tycoon, mirroring the careers of the men around her, most of whom have a hearty contempt for formal education.

Girls in the real-life world of the sociologists, however, are already getting restless in their dead-end jobs. Of the reasons for resignation given by the girls in the study, marriage only occurs in ninth place. The first three reasons are "wished to return to school," "desired a change," and "no future." Marriage may still be their ultimate goal, and provide a better living than the office can do, but even at this early stage, the pretense that the dead-end nature of the work merely reflects the girls' propensity for early marriage obviously doesn't hold up.

In fact, it might be more accurate to say that the office disappointed girls much earlier than has been believed, and that the falling marriage age throughout this century has reflected rather than caused this disappointment.

The twenties were the decade of the exodus from the American farm, which often meant that the younger generation sought work in the nearest large city. Immigrants and ex-farmers swelled the factory population, and the small-town and small-business people who had served the rural areas went into the offices. The father of the white-collar girl was usually a small entrepreneur who was seeing hard times. In spite of his genteel pretensions, he could not support a grown daughter, much less marry her off very well. Her alternatives were teaching or office work, and since the latter meant escaping from home and going to the city, it was the more attractive prospect for a confident girl.

But office work was still not a desirable alternative to marriage, although the contest was more equal in the twenties than it had been in the days of Miss Matfield. Christopher Morley's *Kitty Foyle* was written in 1940, but the story ends in about 1932. The heroine knows that she doesn't have to clutch at matrimonial straws. She gives up her chance of marrying a rich man out of pride—she won't be patronized by his family. She throws herself into her work, and rises from stenographer to traveling promoter of a line of chic cosmetics. She is proud of her independence, and although she still sees the life of a white-collar girl as rougher than marriage, it has its advantages:

> You see, I told Molly, I really did want to say something for them, the WCGs that is, your poor damn share-croppers in the Dust Bowl of business. I see them in subways and on buses, putting up a good fight in their pretty clothes and keeping their heebyjeebies to themselves. There's something so courageous about it, it hurts me inside.
>
> Yes, Molly says, a Pooh-bear on the bedspread isn't enough. If they try to escape by marrying a good provider maybe he's got no brains or he doesn't talk her language. If they marry a man who's smart he may be more interested in his work than he is in her. How are you going to find a man that's both dumb enough and sweet enough?[31]

From a device to rescue the casualties of the marriage battle, women's work in the office is beginning to have some validity of its own. It may be exhausting, but it isn't degrading; a girl may be lonely and broke, but there are definitely worse fates.

So the office girl of the twenties, although she might not be as well off as her married sister, has quite possibly made a choice, and opted for life at work. She has also become a commonplace of the business world; no one can any longer imagine the office without its girl typists. By 1930 the number of girls in offices was greater than the number in factories in the United States, and for the first time office women outnumbered office men.

It was still true that office work led to a very limited liberation. A woman could not earn enough at it to change her position in life or to open up other possibilities. Virginia Woolf, when she wrote in 1928 that a woman must have £500 a year and a room of her own in order to write fiction, certainly did not envisage the woman earning such an amount herself. She reports her own work life, before the arrival of the legacy that enabled her to write:

> I had made my living by cadging odd jobs from newspapers, by reporting a donkey show here or a wedding there; I had earned a few pounds by addressing envelopes, reading to old ladies, making artificial flowers, teaching the alphabet to small children in a kindergarten.[32]

Although there were now more roads into the office, there were just as few roads leading upwards from it. But to the new working girl, with her limited training and few alternatives, the office had its charms. The air of freedom and independence that surrounded going out to work made her attractive to men in an entirely new way. She was livelier and more interesting than the dull, conventional girls who stayed at home.

The flapper of the twenties was often a typist. The first middle-class working girl who had not given up all prospect of attracting men, she was also the first to be contrasted to the "respectable" girls, whether daughters or wives, who were chaperoned through life. Originally, office women had reported to work only when they gave up all hope of masculine support. One and all they were drab old maids, and the fact that they were meeting men unknown to their parents soon ceased to cause alarm. Sequestered in their offices and locked into their dormitories, the price of their employment was the total renunciation of sex appeal.

But once both the girls and the companies realized that female labor was indispensable, the girls stopped worrying about their behavior. They were in a sellers' market, and they could afford to be self-confident and abandon their old servility.

Part of the change was that all through the boom of the twenties, the office was attracting many more girls who could barely claim middle-class status. The new typists were of the class who, in the form of domestic servants and shopgirls, had traditionally provided sexual entertainment for "respectable" men. As they entered the office, the folklore about them followed. Saucy, frivolous, and quickly fading, they were not marriage material for the young executives, but they were often envied by the girls who were.

Rich girls, of course, still didn't work; it was an idea that would never have occurred to Fitzgerald's heroines. (It barely occurred to his heroes.) So although the girls who had the office to themselves were looked down on slightly, and sometimes pitied, there was also the suspicion that they were having a wonderful time. Wives began to be jealous of them, and sheltered girls longed to bob their hair and join them. Movies like *Grand Hotel* showed them, pert and cute, stealing some of the thunder from the stars. They were still "good" girls, who stood no nonsense from men who got "fresh," but there was the quite new implication that they could say "yes" if they wanted to.

This has remained the common image of the office girl, but its piquant fascination has faded as sexual availability has traveled up the social scale. The questions that surrounded these girls, the new social force they represented, has become the commonplace of the urban, bureaucratized world. The girls who achieved some independence through the office interested the serious writers of their day, who were concerned with the whole business of making a living in the new white-collar world. Familiarity with the process has, by now, bred an almost total lack of interest.

In the thirties, the drama of the young girl seeking her fortune in the big city had become a Hollywood cliché. With full Cinderella trappings, it was made into countless movies and popular novels. But the real novelty had gone from the working girl, and in any description of the office world, she was simply there—as irrevocable and uninteresting as the desks and telephones. Even the Depression could not move her—just as in high-unemployment areas today, women could often get office jobs when their husbands were out of work. The number of secretaries and typists continued to rise dramatically, especially in the government bureaucracy set up to deal with the economic crisis.

The fact of the Depression was, however, used to manipulate those women who were trying to move up into important or well-paid jobs. Wherever they were not wanted, the argument that they were taking jobs away from men who had to support families was brought into play. This attitude helped to inaugurate the era that Kate Millett points to as the "counter-revolution" (1930–60). Women had challenged the system sufficiently to gain some new working roles, but only the ones that men wanted them to have. Any further challenge was met with strong resistance.

There were other forces at work during the thirties to bring the new working women to heel. The tide of interest in Freudian psychology was rising in America, and it gave a powerful new weapon to the "woman's place is in the home" school. Now she was not just disruptive if she wanted to get out, nor was she simply taking bread out of the mouths of working men. She was violating her own nature, and heading for neurotic conflict that she would pass on to her children.

The radicalism of the thirties could work both ways. On the one hand, it could be another set of arguments for women's subordination, this time to the revolution or to the common good. Even the Soviet Union, worried about its falling birth rate, went back on its early espousal of easy divorce and abortion. But the climate of freedom and seriousness in the radical movements of the decade did help to create a more independent, sophisticated working girl, who for the first time looked on work as a vehicle for personal liberation in the full sense.

The heroine of Mary McCarthy's novel set in the thirties, *The Company She Keeps*, typifies many of the new feminine attitudes towards work. She has a series of jobs, most of which are secretarial. The product of an Eastern college, with intellectual aspirations, she tells herself that many of her jobs are simply "experience" and a look at other sides of life, the way a thirties writer might have become a vagabond or a taxi driver to learn about life. The jobs keep her going between divorces (and thus provide an alternative to marriage in a entirely new sense). She is known as an independent and slightly intimidating character, and not quite marriageable by someone as respectable as the Yale man with whom she has an affair. She drunkenly tells a man she picks up on the train to Reno,

> "You know what my favorite quotation is? . . . It's from Chaucer . . . Criseyde says it, 'I am myn owene woman, wel at ese.'"
>
> The man had some difficulty in understanding the Middle English, but when at last he had got it straight, he looked at her with bald admiration.
>
> "Golly," he said, "you are, at that!"[33]

Traditional men like this don't altogether know how to take her. She is on her own, and thus must be available; but for all her approachability, she is respectable. You can't think of her as a tart, but what is she? This is a kind of confusion that intellectual, "liberated" women still provoke.

The round of divorces and secretarial jobs begins to pall, but she doesn't start dreaming, as the previous heroines have done, of the true love of a good man. Instead, her psychiatrist advises her that what she really wants is freedom through the self-respect gained from work she is interested in.

> The days of romantic destitution were gone for her. It was no longer possible for her to conceive of herself as a ribbon clerk at Macy's. Now there was not so much time left in the world that you could spend two years or three in the unrewarding occupation of keeping yourself alive. Her apprenticeship was finished. If she took a job, it would have to be a good one, one that would keep the talents limber. No more secretarial

work, no more office routine, that wonderful, narcotic routine that anaesthetizes the spirit, lulls the mind to sleep with the cruel paranoiac delusion of the importance, the value to humanity, of the humble-task-well-done.[34]

One of the implications of this line of thought is that not only can marriage be an escape from work, but work can be an escape from marriage. The alternatives are as clear as they ever were, but which is chosen depends on how much satisfaction each is likely to provide, and marriage is already seen as possibly not fully satisfying to an ambitious girl. This is a complaint that hasn't been heard since it was made by idle wives at the turn of the century; the working girl's longing to escape her dead-end drudgery silenced it for a while, but it is quickly coming back.

The Second World War, like the first, greatly increased the demand for female labor, and put a temporary halt to "woman's place is in the home." Once again, it was "discovered" that her place was where she was needed, and this was now in the factories and offices.

All the single girls, however, were already working. There was only one source of female labor left to draw on—the wives. For the first time, it became respectable, indeed normal, for middle-class married women to go out to work. Working-class wives were already working where necessary, and staying home from the gruelling jobs available to them when possible. The only women who had never worked before were the ones who were likely to end up in the office.

Among working women in 1940, 48 per cent were single and only 31 per cent were married. The Second World War dramatically reversed these proportions. . . . By 1950 the proportion of married women living with their husbands had risen to 48 per cent of all working women while that of single women had fallen to 32 per cent.[35]

Women moved farther up the occupational ladder than they had ever done before, especially in public administration, but their rise was always justified in terms of the country's need. It provided no basis for their continued progress when this need came to an end.

The war years also produced a nostalgia for the home, felt by both men and women. The office, increasingly a female ghetto, seemed drab to its new inhabitants, and men in the army romanticized the picture of the wife and home left behind. Both sexes wanted to take up domestic life where it had been so rudely interrupted.

When the veterans did return, there was strong feeling that they should be given priority over the women who had "filled in" in their absence. The ideal of woman in the home and man at work could now, it was felt, be made a reality again.

Women did not in fact retreat to the home; although there was a leveling off of female office employment immediately after the war, the whole decade of the 1940's shows a massive increase in America—from 5,380,000 to 8,858,000, or from 45 per cent to 52 per cent of white-collar workers. The number grew even faster during the fifties.

The ideology of the home-centered woman was used, then, not to keep women out of work—the postwar boom needed them just as badly as the war had done. Instead, it was used to keep them in the sort of ancillary jobs that they had begun to outgrow during the war. Persuasive propaganda was needed to make women accept their demotion and their renewed lack of opportunity, and this is the reason for the intense propagation of the suburban myth, the consumer myth, the motherhood myth, and the rest of the ideology that trapped Betty Friedan's fellow housewives.

The middle-class women who did live the myth retreated to the suburbs, arguably the most confining existence women have known since purdah, but also the embodiment of the material aspects of the American dream. A boom economy meant that every family could have its own house, car, appliances, lawn, and as many kids as it wanted.

Women who did work justified it in terms of keeping up with the demands of the rising standard of living. Those who did not work were held up as objects of envy. The pressure on the wife to consume was equaled by the pressure on her husband to produce and get ahead. The man in the gray flannel suit was under stress as never before. Business was competitive and ruthless, and the pace increased every year. Executives did not spare themselves in their efforts to keep up with the rat-race—there was no time for anything but work. Evenings, weekends, the long commute on the train—each had its briefcase full of papers.

The wives, off in never-never land with the kids and the station wagon, knew less and less about what went on in the offices of the city. Men's and women's worlds had almost no points of contact. The kids were asleep when Daddy came home.

The wives tried, fruitlessly, to explain the situation to their husbands, who in turn complained that they were slaving every moment so that the wives could live in this split-level paradise. What more could they do?

When the nagging was added to the commuting, the pressure, the mortgage, and the crabgrass, the husbands began coming home later and later. The secretaries, who had held their hands and cheered them up all day, came into their own. Here were girls who knew how rough it was at the office, who didn't give a man a hard time when he wanted to relax, who lived in convenient apartments and had time for drinks after work. They kept themselves looking nice and weren't always worried about children's illnesses and broken washing machines. What's more, they were younger than the wives.

The modern pattern of office romance was established. The wives, often ex-secretaries themselves, knew very well what was happening, and their magazines filled up with stories about "little home-wreckers" who didn't get their man, and loving wives who won their husbands back. Inevitably, each group of women began to envy the other.

The secretaries dreamed of marriage and the luxurious life of the split-level, of the possessions and legitimacy of the wife. The wives dreamed of the glamor of the big city, seductive cocktail lounges, no children, chic bachelor-girl apartments. Neither picture was accurate.

The dreams were especially inaccurate in view of the demographic changes taking place at the office. Although the office girl enshrined in popular mythology was (and still is) single and in her early twenties, after 1950 she was at least as likely to be married, and her average age was rising steeply. The myth of the sexy secretary meant that the most visible girls, those in contact with the public or the boss, were still young, but offices now contained vast tracts of desks and typewriters inhabited by middle-aged women who had returned to work, or wives who had simply never left.

Because of the myth's emphasis on sexy singleness at work, it was still difficult for a girl to envision any life at all for herself after her period of sexual attractiveness was over. She still did not realize just how many years she would work, and for how few of those years she would be eligible for the sort of job that she held in fantasy. When the realization came after a few years at work, the way out was what it had always been—marriage. The enviable life of the mythical secretary was hard to lead after thirty, and so the envy of the office girl for the housewife did not diminish even as the glamor of her role increased.

It was a familiar story for the secretaries to dream of marriage. They had been getting married and leaving work ever since secretarial jobs became the normal way to fill in the few years after high school. This pattern was self-fulfilling, since it provided an excuse for not promoting women, and the lack of opportunity drove them away from the office.

What was new was to find the wives—the safe, comfortable wives, who had found eternal security protected by a living checkbook—envying those driven, haunted, desperate career girls. This pattern had not been seen for decades, ever since the first office women got their much-wanted jobs. But there were lots of reasons why the wives wanted to get back to work.

Marriage was no longer the safe haven it had been. The divorce and desertion rate was rising every year, and some estimates indicated that half of all American marriages failed. If a wife allowed herself to become too dependent, she might find herself trapped and helpless when the walkout came.

A family with just one income wasn't so well off any more. City housing became more and more expensive and decayed; the suburbs sprawled farther out. Inflation struck terror to the hearts of the middle-class millions. A wife who worked was an asset, and public opinion was beginning to swing around to this view.

Disillusionment with the suburbs had set in. The aim of the children nurtured there was to escape their conscientious mothers. Husbands didn't want to come home from the city. Whereas mothers suspected that it would be fun to get out of the ghetto once in a while, their daughters knew very well that they didn't want to be stuck there themselves. The very psychologists who had demanded that mothers spend every moment with their children now found the suburban kids weak, passive, spoilt, and rebellious. They restudied the whole question of working mothers and began to come down on the other side. The girls who had been criticized in the fifties for not using their expensive degrees were now anxious to get to work and stay there.

Perhaps the biggest change of all, the fruit of the other changes, was that the ideology of feminism was reborn. Women who had experienced both the roles open to them, a confining job and a confining home, were not satisfied with either one. They began to realize that the problem was not where they were or what they were doing, but whether they were doing their own thing or someone else's. They began to get suspicious of the whole system that sent them to work when it was convenient and kept them home when it wasn't, that told them they could have the jobs no one else wanted but must move over to make room for any man who chose to challenge their right to these jobs.

The girls who had used the office as a time-filler began to take it seriously and demand more from it. Wives no longer looked on work as a poor second to family-raising; they tried to combine the two in a variety of new ways.

The office had several defenses against the onslaught of the educated wives. It continued to hire young girls wherever possible, and to relegate the wives to routine work. Most of all, it kept up the myth of the sexy secretary, so that middle-aged women felt uncomfortable and out of place in the top secretarial jobs.

The young women coming to the office now looked on their careers as a series of battles. How would they be able to arrange for child care while they were at work? How could they get promoted in spite of prejudice? Should they learn to type or pretend they didn't know how? There was no doubt now about their goal—a good job as well as a family. There was only doubt and disagreement about the best way of reaching it.

In fifty years, office work had become the norm for middle-class women. It was more characteristic of their lives than almost anything else—a woman was likely to spend more years at work than at home with the children. It had taken a long time for this fact to sink in, and much propaganda had been devoted to concealing it and pretending that women were still primarily domestic creatures. The debate about "should women work?" was still heard, long after it had become a resounding irrelevance. But women were no longer listening to it.

The Women's Liberation movement that exploded in the late sixties was, then, the culmination of a whole series of profound changes. If women had not already gone to work, and defined their problem as how to combine their many new roles, they could never have formulated the demands for nurseries and day-care centers, abortions and contraceptives, legal and actual equality, that are now being heard. The long period of apprenticeship, of gaining access to the male world, was a necessary prelude to any attack upon the citadels of power.

Chapter Three
SUBSTITUTE WIVES

THE MOVE OF women to the office has introduced work relationships that mirror family relationships. It has also meant that the status of almost all office men has been raised, rather in the way that the status of American immigrants was raised by each successive wave of immigration.

Such men as still do routine office work are objects of pity rather than aspiration. The writers who used clerical jobs as a respectable, undemanding way to make a living and observe the human race—Lamb, Kafka, Maupassant—have almost all disappeared; those in business at all would now qualify as "executives," like Wallace Stevens in his insurance company. Even in the 1920's, it was considered a major tragedy that T. S. Eliot was forced to work in a bank, and his friends combined to buy him out of it. But the female poet Stevie Smith worked as a secretary in London all her life without a protest from anybody. (This may be one reason why women are today achieving literary eminence in greater numbers than ever before—they are not tempted into high-paying, high-pressure jobs.)

In spite of the sex-typing of office jobs, there is a sense in which life for all office workers is much the same. Office work is much too common nowadays to carry any cachet; but the range of attitudes to it is as wide as the range of human temperament itself. Two characters in a recent novel called *The Office* exemplify the extreme points of view:

> I *was* free. And then suddenly they shut you up for eight hours every day. Eight hours in a small box. No wonder I cried. And it's far worse than prison. It's not a punishment—it's your reward! This eight by ten box is your reward for passing exams, doing what you were told, trying hard to please. Your reward is to sit in that box for the rest of your life.[1]

The man who enjoys the office responds:

I don't really *like* too much real life any more. I'm quite ready to admit it. In the office you get little dramas, little friendships, little loves and hates. With one or two additions which we won't go into, my entire emotional life is satisfied here.

LAWRENCE: But, Peter—the *work*. I enjoy a bit of gossip as much as the next man. But the appalling triviality of the work; the monotony of it, the undemandingness of it. You might as well spend the rest of your life . . . I don't know . . . piling up pins or something. Balancing tiddly-winks in heaps. . . . the endless competition, the struggling to get approval, the degrading sucking-up. The stupid battles to get one's way. The ruthlessness.

—PETER: Not in Specifications, ducky. And who's ruthless in Packaging and Design? No-one's been sacked for fifteen years. In America perhaps. Not here. It was even better before the war I don't doubt, but it's still Arcadia. . . . It's like tapestry; time passes, the mind is active or drifts, distant sounds of—you know—the tinkle of the tea trolley, the ping of a typewriter bell.[2]

But although the office is in some ways a microcosm of the outside world, there are very definite limits on what it includes—and these limits are the source of much of what people like and dislike about the office.

Adults of both sexes are now included in the office, but mainly women between sixteen and thirty and men between twenty-five (sometimes a bit younger) and sixty-five. Only those who are literate, and middle-class in appearance and manners, are usually allowed. In some offices, of course, the range is much narrower—the identically suited I.B.M. executives are an extreme example, as are the ladies in the offices of *Vogue*. The limits of appearance in most offices do not stretch to include extreme bohemianism (kaftans, bare feet) or extreme dowdiness (dirty work clothes, aprons). Americans who grew up in jeans and sneakers often rail against the conformity of the office, because adopting a new uniform in place of the old seems to them an imposition. They mustn't be too different from each other to be able to get along.

Thus, the office is an escape from the turmoil and variety of the streets outside, especially in a large, chaotic city. People are not preselected as stringently as they are for, say, a university, but the screening process is usually rigorous enough to permit friendships among most of the people who pass it.

The office rigidly excludes the trappings of domestic life, usually on the grounds that it is "unbusinesslike" and would impair the workers' efficiency. Children are almost never seen there. Too obvious domesticity—extensive lunch-hour grocery shopping, phone calls home—is frowned upon as indicating escapism, disloyalty, and lack of interest in the work. Any distractions related to work—hair-dos, clothes shopping, lunches with co-workers—are looked on more leniently as evidence of a desire to appear smart and interested in the office.

Thus, the office, by permitting only that frivolity which is based on narcissism, places itself firmly in the courtship period of life when personal adornment is the overriding interest, before the advent of diapers and sofas. This is why young women seem most at home there, and why men so much enjoy escaping to the office world. Responsible as they may be there, they are free of domestic responsibility. They are young again.

Middle-aged office women are notorious growers of desk plants, decorators of walls, pinners-up of family photographs. It is hard for them to avoid the nest-making instinct that has been encouraged in them all their lives. But all women try, in one way or another, to sabotage the office atmosphere of functional furniture, drab walls, and sterile filing cabinets. Simone de Beauvoir has given a reason for this.

> The office universe . . . this universe of formalities, of absurd gestures, of purposeless behavior, is essentially masculine. Woman gets her teeth more deeply into reality; for when the office worker has drawn up his figures, or translated boxes of sardines into money, he has nothing in his hands but abstractions. The baby fed and in his cradle, clean linen, the cooking, constitute more tangible assets. . . . Man's enterprises are at once projects and evasions: he lets himself be smothered by his career and his "front"; he often becomes self-important,

serious. Being against man's logic and morality, woman does not fall into these traps.[3]

Liberationists would no doubt prefer to substitute a phrase like "people who have been confined to a domestic role" for "woman," and "people who have been defined by work roles" for "man." This quibble aside, Beauvoir analyzes neatly the problem of why women continue to try to establish a personal beachhead in the impersonal office, in the face of the ridicule and contempt of their more "practical" colleagues.

Everyone knows about these aspects of office behavior. But new light has been shed on the office by applying the findings of the ethologists, who have described patterns of territorial division and status-ranking among animals. In the office, as in the jungle, increased confidence and aggressiveness are shown near the center of one's territory (near one's own desk), and insecurity increases with the distance away (when called in to see the boss, for example). Leaning or sitting uninvited on someone else's desk is cause for real hostility, and the desk forms a protective barrier for the person behind it. A sign of friendliness in an interview is for the interviewer to come around to the same side of the desk as the interviewee; a sign of suspicion, even hostility, is for him to preserve his desk-barrier rigidly, even at the end of the talk.

Less well-known is the importance of "conceptual space"—the connection between the size of the work area and the size of the ideas that come from it. Social historian Anthony Christie believes that

> the longer an individual is in a situation of relative restraint, that is the space in which he works is constricted and too small, the more likely is his adaptation to the circumstances to become irreversible. Potential executives and managers may well be lost by overlong exposure in physical environments where the area available of personal space is too little for their proper development.[4]

It has recently been shown that women tend to receive the same proportion of office space as they do of pay—20 per cent to 50 per cent less than that of men doing roughly the same work in the same office. This may well be related to management's inability to find potential executives among them.

Permission to have an individual desk arrangement is also a sign of status and of high expectations by the management. "Creative" people in advertizing agencies are notorious for their office decor—they may choose to work in a prison cell, a discotheque, a gym, or a chateau. At the other extreme, the philosophy behind the open-plan office is that it ensures uniform work with no slacking, since it is harder to read or knit in the open than in the privacy of a cubicle.

The drab office that cannot be changed by any amount of effort is depressing. But possibly even more of a strain for the workers is the glossy, decorator office, which must not bear any sign of the personalities of those who work there. The personality of the decorator is the only one allowed. Companies that go in for expensive, uniform office furniture often go in for expensive, uniform office girls—the frumpy old typists are replaced by glossy new receptionists. Eating, chatting, even smoking are forbidden, and pin-ups of Paul Newman are ruthlessly suppressed. The typing is expected to be impeccable.

The higher the concentration of women in a particular area of the office, the lower the standard of decor. The "mixed" areas are next; and the smartest are usually the men-only bastions: the board room, the executive lounge, the theater for "presentations." This reflects the distribution of women at the bottom of the corporate ladder. The Bank of America, for instance, has a staff of 39,341—28 per cent male and 72 per cent female. The number of managers is 7,171—77 per cent male and 23 per cent female: a fairly exact reversal of the percentages.

This status-ranking extends not only to office decor. It pervades every aspect of the company's treatment of its employees. The expectations are different at different levels, and, not surprisingly, the performance of the workers tends to reflect what is expected of them.

Even the games played by the efficiency experts, consultants, and psychologists are different on each floor of the building. The problem of motivation among the managers is tackled as a question of incentives—it is assumed that the young men are eager to be allowed to shoulder responsibility and take risks, and the only problem is that not everyone in the company can advance as fast as he would like. A company with too much young talent is in trouble: massive resignations must be expected when the young men get fed up with waiting for their chance. A company with too many key positions sewn up by ageing executives is warned by the experts: where will the young men see their future? Recruiters are warned that the eager graduates they pursue are not interested in rhetoric, but in results; that they will leave the most well-intentioned company if they find themselves stuck in a dead-end.

Managers are selected and trained for their "male" qualities—aggressiveness, toughness, practicality. As one critique of "businessmen's style" points out, "Jobs must be tackled, objections overruled, problems attacked, difficulties overcome, and offensives must always be seized."[5]

The managerial ego is nurtured and encouraged to such an extent that it sometimes becomes a positive handicap to the running of the business. Outside experts must be called in to devise ways of making the superstars more cooperative without arousing too much hostility. This allows one man to criticize another's ideas without starting a full-scale guerrilla war. British American Tobacco gingerly adopted such a program:

> In a company that is trying to . . . introduce a more democratic style any device that unfreezes the rigid boss/subordinate relationship and enables managers to talk more freely and frankly with one another has its advantages. . . . BAT was somewhat nervous of involving real life bosses and subordinates in the exercise. It feared that either nothing at all would happen because the subordinates would be too scared of really saying what they thought of the boss. Or that too much would happen and that the outburst would irretrievably rupture a carefully established working relationship.[6]

The assumptions that these companies make about managerial men—that they are tough, aggressive, but sensitive to slights—

obviously reflect the way they want the managers to perform. By taking their ambition seriously, the company can help to make them ambitious; by expecting them to fight for their preserves of power, it encourages the fighting instinct that can then be turned against competitors. By expecting confident performance from the men, it makes them more confident in themselves.

Conversely, the company's expectations of its women also tend to be fulfilled. If it expects them to leave after a year, leave they do; if it expects them to be apathetic and uninterested, so they are. In any case, their problems are usually seen as less rarefied and difficult to solve than those of the managers. Another "expert" solution to a personnel problem illustrates this very neatly. The Bell Telephone Company consulted the famous Fred Herzberg to see if he could raise productivity in their customer complaints division. The company

> introduced Herzbergian techniques to enrich the jobs of the girls it employed to handle complaints. . . . Instead of copying out a standard answer the girls were encouraged to use their own words and to draft a reply themselves. At the same time the load on supervisors was reduced. Instead of checking each reply as a matter of routine they were only called in when the girl felt she had a problem on which she needed advice. As a result the jobs of both the girls and the supervisors became more interesting; the girls responded to the challenge of greater responsibility and the supervisors, after a certain amount of apprehension, were relieved of a great deal of drudgery.[7]

The big surprise to the company was obviously that the girls responded to stimuli like "responsibility"—in other words, the sort of carrots usually saved to be dangled in front of managers. The companies that overrate the complexity and capability of their men tend to systematically underrate their women—until they have to hire an expert to tell them that girls selected for their literacy can be permitted to "use their own words."

This experiment is a scathing indictment of a large company's inability to make full use of its employees' talents. It is not even oppressing them in the name of efficiency; the revised work plan saved $558,000 in one year.

Just as an atmosphere of low expectation can stifle the routine office worker, the atmosphere of importance, complete with jargon and mystification, obviously helps the executive to get through his day. The status symbols of management and the respect of his employees are important to his self-esteem; any change in the status quo is as much of a blow to his ego as would be a challenge to his position as head of his family.

All these patterns—the undervaluing of female labor, the sharp differentiation of sex roles, the status gradations based on age and sex—are the mirror-image of family life. It is, however, a curious kind of family life, changing more slowly than the real family and embodying male fantasies of how the family should be.

Analysts of modern marriage say that it is ceasing to be "complementary"—that is, each partner having a unique role—and becoming more "symmetrical," with both partners doing the same things and "filling in" for each other. But this pattern has yet to reach the office. How very conservative the office is can be seen immediately in its dress—the continuing force of patriarchy is enshrined in dark suits and ties, neat little dresses, careful make-up. All this is in direct contrast to the modern world outside, where, according to fashion historian James Laver, "We are at the end of a patriarchal system. Men no longer have to give the impression of being good providers by their dress, nor women of being good mothers and housekeepers." The office's hostility to female trousers is another indication of its unwillingness to see any erosion in the traditional sex roles.

If the office is a family, it is definitely a large Victorian family that includes domestic servants as well as wives, mothers, and daughters. The atmosphere may at times be that of the disintegrating large family described in the novels of Ivy Compton-Burnett, where thoughts of murder, incest, and escape lurk just under the repressive surface. Certainly it is rarely, these days, the jolly Dickensian hearthside scene.

Historically, many office routines were taken over from Victorian household routines. The secretary not only plays the roles of women in the family and servants, but even of the social secretary of that time. *The Social Secretary,* published in 1919, describes the tasks of the "visiting amanuensis." She is to hire and supervise the house servants, pay them, keep the household accounts, sort the mail, pay the bills, and answer letters (herself or from dictation). She also sends and records invitations and keeps the engagement-book.[8]

Today's secretary also acts as wife, mother, mistress, and maid, on successive days, at different stages in her career, or with different bosses. This is why it is hard to decide whether, at any one time, she is an office wife or an office household servant.

Another reason why all the roles acted out by Victorian women seem to have blurred in the modern office is that they have blurred in modern life as well. Each man has many fewer women to serve him, and a wife today (or a secretary) is likely to combine many functions. But each woman is still jealous of her prestige, which makes her hostile to the man's other female helpers and anxious to dissociate herself from them. Although the jobs of wives and secretaries are similar, and often overlap, they themselves are conscious of the distinction. The wife, in particular, sees it as a distinction between herself and a servant.

Veblen has described the role of wives, however, in terms that are today applicable also to secretaries.

> The leisure rendered by the wife . . . is, of course, not a simple manifestation of idleness or indolence. It almost invariably occurs disguised under some form of work or household duties or social amenities, which prove on analysis to serve little or no ulterior end beyond showing that she does not and need not occupy herself with anything that is gainful or that is of substantial use.[9]

What the secretary does can well be described as "household duties or social amenities," and the higher the standing of her boss, the less real use she has to be. The same is true of the wife.

There is one way in which the secretary has a higher value even than the wife; she has been specially trained for the role.

Domestic service might be said to be spiritual rather than a mechanical function. Gradually there grows up an elaborate system of good form, specifically regulating the manner in which this vicarious leisure of the servant class is to be performed. Any departure from these canons of form is to be deprecated, not so much because it evinces a short-coming in mechanical efficiency, or even that it shows an absence of the servile attitude and temperament, but because, in the last analysis, it shows the absence of special training . . . trained service has utility . . . as putting in evidence a much larger consumption of human service than would be shown by the mere present conspicuous leisure performed by an untrained person.[10]

Secretarial skills like shorthand obviously represent this kind of value; a highly-trained girl, whether or not her skills are necessary, has more prestige value than an untrained one.

It is, of course, only the wives of the leisure class that Veblen is talking about. So emulating them, for a secretary who is likely to be lower middle class in origin, represents a definite increase in prestige. It is more valuable in status terms for a secretary to learn the skills of these wives—Cordon Bleu cooking, conversation about the arts, sophisticated dress—than for her to learn even the most difficult secretarial skills.

The basis of the wife's scorn for the secretary is that the wife is usually of a higher class. The secretary's scorn for the wife, where it exists, is based on the secretary's greater utility. Thus, the thing that each most prizes in herself is exactly what awakens contempt in the other.

The wife-secretary relationship thus mirrors the wife-servant one. It also mirrors the wife-"other-woman" relationship. Being lower on the social scale, secretaries are thought to be more generally sexually available to men of the executive class than are women of the wives' level. This idea is reflected in the thinking of many men: "I wouldn't want my wife to go out to work" often means "I wouldn't want other men thinking about my wife the way I know they think about the girls in the office."

The complex relationships among these female roles—wife,

secretary, servant, mistress—are further complicated by women's work patterns. The ideology described by Veblen still exists in the minds of many men, but it no longer corresponds to social reality. One man's wife, if she's not another man's secretary, may well be his servant. Viola Klein speaks of

> the definite shift in occupations which takes place among women after marriage. While office work of various descriptions absorbs about one-third of the single women, that is, far more than any other kind of employment, domestic work ranks first among married women (31 per cent of the total).[11]

Domestic work is not only easier to fit in with a wife's own household commitments, but her husband may well find it more acceptable than office work for her—it doesn't involve contact with other men.

The jobs of wives and secretaries parallel each other very closely, as we have seen, and yet there is unceasing hostility between them. The wives' magazines print stories about home-wrecking secretaries who unscrupulously use sex to get men away from their families; the secretaries' magazines print stories about nagging, frumpy, spendthrift wives who exhaust and exploit their hard-working husbands, who naturally turn to the understanding, helpful secretaries for comfort (the secretaries invariably suffering in silence as they send the strengthened men back to their appalling families). "If only she knew that I'm really the one who saved her marriage...."

Each secretly believes that she has the best or most real part of the man—the wife because she bears his children and his name and sleeps with him, the secretary because she sees him for most of his waking hours and shares his business problems, which often seem more interesting and real to him than do the domestic ones. The preference many men feel for the office, with its aura of youth and its clearly limited demands, is often interpreted by both women as a preference for the secretary over the wife.

Each woman has a set of duties which she jealously guards and considers more important than those allotted to the other woman. Each considers the other's tasks degrading, although they are remarkably similar to her own. For instance:

The Wife	*The Secretary*
Packs his suitcase	Makes his plane reservations
Protects him from the children	Protects him from his subordinates
Pays the household bills	Does his expense account
Sends Christmas cards	Sends Christmas cards
Listens to his office problems	Listens to his domestic problems

A man could get into serious trouble by asking his secretary to dash off a note to his mother or by asking his wife to let them know he'll be late for a meeting. Each would say, "Who do you think I am—your servant?"

The more elevated the executive, the more closely his secretary's duties approximate those of a wife. One manual lists the duties of a "private secretary":

(a) Receive visitors and, if necessary, turn them politely away.

(b) Receive and give messages verbally or by telephone, sufficiently understanding their significance to be able to judge whether or not the message has been correctly passed.

(c) Compose routine replies to letters and memoranda, such as, for example, simple acknowledgements.

(d) Punctuate and correct grammar in transcribing dictation.

(e) Maintain a filing system.

(f) Keep an engagement book, and see that the appointments are kept or some other suitable action taken.

(g) Operate a reminder system, to see that jobs which the executive should do at some future date are, in fact, dealt with at the correct time.[12]

The secretary in all this is a cipher, as invisible as possible. These are not *her* messages that are being passed on; the appointments in the engagement book are not to be kept by her. The executive, whose time is so valuable that he cannot even receive his own visitors, is obviously an ungrammatical, forgetful, helpless boob. If this secretary were a wife, she might well complain of being taken for granted, or even of mental cruelty.

The secretary-wife is all too likely to be treated the way only the unluckiest wives are treated. But playing the wifely role has other drawbacks as well. Not only is she practically invisible, but when the boss does notice her it is as a dreary reminder of duty and of the passage of time. She loses all the excitement that once made her practically the "other woman." If she ever had an aura of tempting independence, she doesn't now.

An Englishman once described the public-school fagging system, which assigns younger boys as servants to older boys, in these terms: "You would really be more likely to have sex with almost any other boy than with your fag. After all, he's like a wife, and who wants sex with his wife?" It's this mentality, carried over into adult life, that makes the wifely role such a dreary one for the secretary to play.

The real wife, in compensation, has the edge over the secretary in legitimacy, permanence, and status. An obvious proof of this is that a secretary who marries the boss is considered to have reached a desirable goal.

The wife is a more conspicuous consumer because every aspect of her existence reflects on her husband—ideally, she should have a big house, expensive clothes, servants, a car. The secretary should look smart, but it's irrelevant that she lives in a one-room slum and takes the bus to work. She may go along on a few business trips and important dinners, but the wife will go much more often. (This may not always be the boss's choice. An airline that offered free fares to wives on business trips sent out a questionnaire to ask the wives how they enjoyed it. The wives all replied, "What trip?")

The secretary has only one power game to play—the sweetness-and-deference one. Things are more complicated in the family; even the weakest marriage is longer-lasting than a work partnership, and much harder to get out of. Wives can use money, sex, the children, bad temper, and an almost infinite number of other weapons to get their way, but insecurity keeps the secretary sweet.

This may be another reason why secretaries are currently less given to complaining about their lives than are wives. Not only can they get out of it more easily, they can also be made to get out. "Personality clash" is considered in most offices a valid reason for firing a secretary, as is "uncooperative" or "negative attitude." No wonder secretaries often seem like goody-goodies, and why they give their boss a deference that he usually doesn't get at home.

On the other hand, the position of the secretary-mistress is probably stronger than ever before. Wives are still more permanent, but they are nothing like as permanent as they used to be. Men don't hide their mistresses in back streets any more—they flaunt them in chic restaurants. Far from being shameful, an affair with an attractive woman is a matter of pride, and the concept of the "fallen woman" has become ludicrous.

No matter how the balance of power shifts between wife and secretary, one strong bond remains: their work. Office work is still the business equivalent of housekeeping, even if secretaries are not always office wives.

Both jobs are custodial, concerned with tidying up, putting away, and restoring order rather than with producing anything. Simone de Beauvoir's description of housework is just as applicable to office work:

> Few tasks are more like the torture of Sisyphus than housework, with its endless repetition: the clean becomes soiled, the soiled is made clean, over and over, day after day. The housewife wears herself out marking time: she makes nothing, simply perpetuates the present. She never senses conquest of a positive Good, but rather indefinite struggle against a negative Evil.... Washing, ironing, sweeping, ferreting out fluff from under wardrobes—all this halting of decay is also the denial of life; for time simultaneously creates and destroys, and only its negative aspect concerns the housekeeper.[13]

Office work, too, is routine and repetitive. Filing is like washing the dishes, and induces the same sense of frustration. Typing a perfect letter is as transient an achievement as cooking an egg. These things are done with little conscious attention; the routine becomes automatic, and the mind wanders into its own escapist paths, which are different for the secretary and the housewife only because of their different ages and circumstances—the secretary may dream of peace and the wife of distraction; the secretary of a man to fill her life and the housewife of life without her man.

Both kinds of work take place when the master is away; most of his presence is spent giving orders for the next round of work. The tasks are performed on his behalf but do not depend on him personally—that is, he creates the need for the shirts to be ironed and the typing to be done; there would be neither typing nor shirts without him, but who he is doesn't matter—the creation of these tasks is common to every husband and every boss.

The "personal touches" added by the wife and secretary are overrated by the woman and scarcely noticed by the man; if they intrude on his attention at all, they are likely to be an annoyance —"Why can't my socks always be in the same place?" or "How do you expect me to find anything on this desk?" To her, the idea is to magnify the importance of the task; to him, the idea is to get it done as quickly and unobtrusively as possible.

Mechanical contrivances do not lessen the time spent on such work, but only raise the standard that is to be reached. It is by now well established that washing machines, vacuum cleaners, mixers, and dishwashers do not cut down the time the average housewife spends on her tasks; these things simply mean that she does more laundry, cleans more thoroughly, cooks more elaborate meals, and spends a lot of time fussing with the machines and waiting for the repairman. The only things that do make a difference to her routine are the number and age of her children and the amount of money that she has to spend on gadgetry. When there are one or two babies, she stops getting out the silver teapot when the neighbors come, not to begin again until she is middle-aged and once more comparatively idle.

The magazines that sold her the "labor-saving" machines also sold her the idea that "nothing says lovin' like something from the oven," that she can achieve the whiter white, and that her bathroom is harboring unseen germs. She may not have to clean the grate with blacking, or boil the laundry on the stove, but she cannot lag behind in interior decoration, gourmet cooking, or grooming to keep her husband. Competitive housework has replaced drudgery, and represents her futile search for a tangible achievement in life.

Meanwhile, back at the office, perfectionism goes from height to height. The computer spews forth ever more information about sales, profits, productivity. These results must be analyzed and incorporated into future plans. Each meeting must have a perfectly typed agenda, with all the last-minute corrections included. The customers' letters must emerge immaculate from the new electric typewriter, and if a girl really wants to shine in her boss's eyes, not even one erasure must be permitted.

The new office furniture has such clean modern lines that file folders must never be left on top of the cabinet; papers must never litter the desk; even a cup of coffee should be hidden if a superior visitor arrives. Staples must never be used to attach enclosures to letters; they break the new postage machine. Reports that used to be passed from hand to hand are now Xeroxed so that each member of the committee can have a copy. Requisition forms must now be filled out for everything, since the efficiency experts discovered that stationery was being wasted. They didn't look in the wastebasket to see the five spoilt copies of an important letter that had to be perfect.

The secretary's search for perfection, like the housewife's, can only be curtailed by the arrival of a more important job. A girl who has spent two hours every day doing the filing can dispose of it in five minutes if she is asked to try her hand at drafting a memo. Bosses who realize this use higher-level work to tempt the secretary into speeding up her routine; so he gets two jobs done for the time and the price of one.

But the secretary can't always control the proliferation of her work. As a housewife whose husband gets promoted has a bigger house to keep clean and more elaborate dinner parties to serve, the secretary must keep up with the flood of paperwork that lands on his desk. He can no longer be expected to care for the garden, which is now an acre instead of a patch of lawn; nor can he read the reports that demand his initials. They must be digested for him and presented in capsule form. Massive reports must be summarized in one page or less; he must be briefed for the meeting in five minutes. So of course there's no time for him to work on his own report; he must simply approve a draft prepared by his secretary, who in turn sends it to the typing pool. The high-powered office, like the large household, needs a big supporting staff.

Both the wife and the secretary mainly have just to "be there." They are the guardians, the custodians, the stavers-off of possible disaster. The wife can't leave—"What if the house caught fire? What if the children got sick?" Nor can the secretary—"What if someone wants to know where Mr. Smith is? What if the phone rings?" Usually the disaster doesn't happen; the female hostage might even be glad if it did.

How much of each job is really necessary is a difficult question, but one that is increasingly being asked. One can no more say that a businessman doesn't need a secretary to answer his phone than one can say that an army doesn't need polished brass buttons, or that a society woman doesn't need a hairdresser. Conspicuous consumption and keeping up with the Joneses can be defended, but too often they are defended on a false basis.

However these jobs are defined, the fact remains that a lot of unpleasant drudgery has to be done in the office and at home, and attempts to say it's unnecessary simply erode the position of those who have to do it. Instead of thinking of creative ways to get it done, society has for the most part silently pushed it onto those least able to get out of it. As Juliet Mitchell points out, "Far from woman's *physical* weakness removing her from productive work, her *social* weakness has ... made her the major slave of it."[14]

Thoughts of liberation have occurred to the housewife more often so far than to the secretary; the level of debate about housework might provide some clues to what will be heard about the typing if liberation ever gets to the office. The remarks recorded by Pat Mainardi in "The Politics of Housework" may soon be heard among the filing cabinets:

> "I don't mind sharing the housework, but I don't do it very well. We should each do the things we're best at."
> Meaning: "I don't like the dull stupid boring jobs, so you should do them."[15]

The usual male defense is, of course, that his time is far too valuable to be wasted on the trivia of day-to-day organization and maintenance. His mind is occupied with the long-term course of the business, and everyone's prosperity rests on his shoulders. But the trivial details that he scorns are as necessary to the functioning of the business as are his own clever ideas. A strike of secretaries, or of wives, would quickly make him aware of this. At the moment, the only time he thinks about the clerical slavery on which he depends is when it is going badly; then he fulminates against the agencies who are inflating the girls' salaries, or the schools that don't teach them to type, or their flightiness and silliness. Having to concentrate for five minutes on the tasks his secretary does all day seems to him an incredible waste of his time.

This is just like the husband's attitude to the housework on which he depends: "I was just finishing this when my husband came in and asked what I was doing. Writing a paper on housework. Housework? he said, *Housework?* Oh my god how trivial can you get. A paper on housework."[16]

The element of drudgery is not the only similarity between housework and office work. Rigid conventions of all kinds have grown up around the performance of office work, until today it is almost as inefficient as traditional housekeeping. The demands of prestige and privacy mean that each housewife and each secretary perform the same tasks in their separate cubicles, and pooling—whether of typing or child care—is resisted.

The housewife particularly has been the victim of that middle-class ideology of privacy which has today spread to vast masses of society and which has made "keeping oneself to oneself" one of the essential virtues in the accepted code of middle-class and lower middle-class proprieties.[17]

The retention of shorthand in spite of its inefficiency is a consequence of the same ideology. It preserves the personal contact that girls value in their jobs, and it is a skill that provides the companies with a selection technique. Bosses like the whole routine of dictating, as it is flatteringly known. In fact, girls are reluctant to take jobs where mechanical equipment is too much used, because their skills will grow rusty. Many practice in the evenings, with the radio or television, after transcribing from the dictaphone all day.

There are many other examples of Veblenesque duties in the office. Typing, for example, is the modern equivalent of embroidery, as a feminine time-filler indicative of conspicuous leisure. It keeps the hands busy without occupying the mind, and standards of skill and perfection are applied to it for their own sake. Modern feminists are appalled at the museums that show old-fashioned needlework implying hours of female frustration and boredom. But what of the files of neatly typed reports, letters, documents of all kinds, all copied from perfectly legible originals? They are equally monuments of busywork.

Colette illustrates the old-fashioned attitude towards sewing, and her modern response to it:

> "Do you mean to say your daughter is nine years old," said a friend, "and she doesn't know how to sew? She really must learn to sew . . ."
>
> She has therefore learned to sew. . . . Then my friends applaud: "Just look at her! Isn't she good? That's right! Your mother must be pleased!"
>
> Her mother says nothing—great joys must be controlled. But ought one to feign them? I shall speak the truth: I don't much like my daughter sewing.[18]

The stories of fledgling secretaries typing a letter five times until it is flawless, of bosses sending back to be redone papers with one thumbprint, are as bizarre in their way as stories of little girls learning to take ten stitches to the inch. But "learn to type" is as common an admonition to today's young girls as "learn to sew" used to be.

Typing has even been fitted into a girl's conventional expectations—work, then marriage—in a way that recalls the era of sewing. As each stitch in the linen used to bring her that much closer to a completed trousseau, each page of type now means another penny in the house or furniture fund.

It is important for a secretary to keep up the appearance of being busy, by typing endlessly or creating a complicated office routine for herself. True idleness, which is occasionally tolerated among wives, is never tolerated in secretaries. Men accuse each other of having idle secretaries as a way of denigrating each other's importance. The middle-level man says, confidentially, "Of course, all the work is really done down here; those fellows up on the sixth floor with their three-martini lunches are just window-dressing." The top brass, on the other hand, unanimously agree, "All those junior executives just think they need secretaries, and we've got to keep them happy. But of course that's why it's so hard to find a good girl nowadays." True idleness is only found in the office backwaters inhabited by ageing women, or in the pools of young girls. Both can escape male scrutiny much more easily than the secretary.

Secretaries, whether they play the part of wives or not, are far from the only women to be found in offices today. In fact, the office can exhibit a far greater variety of female roles than can the average family. It is indeed Victorian in its rambling structure, which has a niche for just about everyone.

Maiden aunts, for example, are as rare as unicorns in actual households, but they can still be found floating around the office, slightly fussy and needing to be shielded from the harsher facts of life, but nice old souls all the same, who listen to people's troubles and keep supplies of goodies in their desks. This role is a good one for any woman who is too old for the sexual game and needs a way to "explain" her slightly anomalous presence. She is easy to accept on this unthreatening basis.

The little maids who were surreptitiously pinched and fondled by Victorian sons have also moved to the office, where they are referred to as "just a little typist." Flirtation with them is perfectly permissible, but slightly degrading, and a man who gets a reputation for it may be treated with mild contempt.

The older, usually single, secretaries who overprotect and infantilize their bosses are the nannies. They have a special position in the firm, and aren't expected to fraternize too much with the other servants. They say, "Well, really he needs someone like me. I'm very tidy, and he'd never be able to find anything if I didn't sort it out for him." Or "Well, you see, he travels a lot, and someone has to make sure he has the right papers in his briefcase and a hotel booked at the other end." Or even, "I don't know wh t would have happened to his marriage by now if he didn't have a secretary. He never thinks to ring up when he's going to be late." They indulge their bosses in every way, while complaining loudly and insincerely about inconsiderateness, lateness, absent-mindedness.

Some of them may even overstep the mark far enough to become positively maternal. The middle-aged secretary who sees the boss, however old he is, as her son is likely to indulge in the same kind of maternal bullying, mixed with a sort of flirtatious deference, as the real middle-aged mum. In the way that a mother will pretend that her son is her "escort," and ask his advice at the same time as she babies him with his favorite dishes, the secretary will fuss over her boss's desk arrangement, pretend that she thinks he is flirting with her, and tease him about his new haircut. She will obstruct anyone who wants to see him, and be particularly hostile to new, young secretaries, just as if they were women "after" her son.

But whatever the role a woman plays at work, she gets her status and power from the patronage of a man in the way described by Mills:

> ... in an almost masochistic way, people may be gratified by subordination on the job ... office women in lower positions of authority are liable to identify with men in higher authority, transferring from prior family connections or projecting to future family relations.[19]

Christiane Collange, in *Madame and Management*,[20] has pretended to believe that wives are more like their husbands than they are like their husbands' secretaries—that they apply management techniques to the household as men do to the office. But this is true only in the most lavish and sophisticated households (like her own—she is a magazine editor and the sister of Servan-Schreiber). In such cases, the secretary, too, will act like a manager. Their roles will still be comparable. And their work, as women, will still be dependent on the resources and status of the man who employs them.

In fact, all the womanly roles we have been discussing—wife, secretary, servant—are aspects of the same role. Any woman who thinks she is escaping her fate either by going out to the office or retreating to the home is simply fooling herself.

In spite of the variety of female roles in the office, the fact remains that statistically, it is a place of young women, or at least women younger than the female population generally. The ideal office is young, sexy, and has a high turnover to keep it that way, and there are some very cogent reasons why this pattern is encouraged by the company.

As Juliet Mitchell points out, the two groups of women who *don't* work are the affluent housewives, particularly those without much education, and the mothers of young children. The absence of the first contributes to the low expectations of working women: as long as some housewives do not work, the ones who do will always feel that they are the ones who have failed, by not making it to the haven of male support. It also deprives the female work force of many of the women who would be most active in trying to change its status—women who would certainly not put up with the lowly jobs and paltry pay offered to women now.

The absence of the second group, young mothers, also works against the interests of working women as a whole. Among "career" women, the period of child-care takes away their crucial years of establishing themselves and winning promotions. Once a woman falls behind in her twenties and thirties, it is no use telling her that she has another thirty years of useful life—she has missed the boat, as any middle-aged male job hunter would testify.

Among working-class women, these years are the ones that should see the rise of political consciousness and an interest in unionism, as they do in men. It is the age when a worker begins to take his job conditions and prospects seriously, and to think about ways of bettering them. A fifteen-year-old girl hasn't developed this consciousness; nor has a mother returning to work after her children are in school. She, too, has missed the crucial stage in her development as a worker.

In the office, the elimination of these two groups of women is accomplished not only by the "natural" pattern of female lives, but by subtle manipulation of the idea of the office as a sexual arena. The secretarial period in a girl's life is arranged to correspond with her period of sexual eligibility, and any deviation from this pattern is made to seem outré.

The myth of the sexy secretary is eagerly propagated by everyone in the office. The newspapers that use it as a source of escapist copy don't realize how many functions it serves. The management certainly realizes it, although their recognition of these functions is usually obscured under layers of verbiage.

First of all, it keeps the secretaries young. This keeps pay raises and overt discontent to a minimum. Much as managements complain about the marriage turnover and the job-hopping of young girls, they connive in it and make it inevitable. Where nonsecretarial opportunities do exist for ambitious girls, they are carefully hidden from most of the secretarial group. Girls are often told when they take secretarial jobs that they must not expect promotion; and some companies keep women out of the higher levels just so that the secretaries will not become discontented.

Even where companies do not officially discourage ambition, the whole climate of the office works against it. Older women are made to feel superfluous and out of place, and their firing or persecution is justified on the grounds that the men like working with younger women, or that the atmosphere of the typing pool is so young and gay it's a shame to spoil it. Just at the point where an older woman may feel that she's ready for the promotion and the raise she has worked towards for so long, she suddenly becomes an embarrassment to the management, and is shunted into a backwater—the library or ordering paperclips.

When she is allowed to stay in her old job, a much younger man is put over her. He feels resentful of her presence, she tries to sabotage him in every way, and the rest of the employees sympathize with him.

The process by which the pretty young secretary becomes the "old bag" is sudden, ruthless, and final. If she stays in one job for too long, she begins to be pitied—why isn't she married yet? Perhaps she has affairs that are known about in the office, perhaps she doesn't—if she does, soon she has "been around" and is talked about contemptuously by the men. If she doesn't, she is pitied— "Poor Sally, by this time she'll probably never get over her fear of men." If she is attractive, signs of decay are anxiously watched for—"She used to be so pretty. I think she's become hard, don't you?" If she makes no effort to attract, she becomes a standing joke—"I'd rather make it with Eleanor Roosevelt." If she is well liked, the subject isn't mentioned—in conversation with her, people are careful not to refer to the length of time she's been there, or what her holiday plans are, or anything else that might highlight her embarrassing condition of manlessness.

Of course, this is nothing more nor less than what happens to ageing spinsters everywhere in our society. People become kind rather than genuinely interested. She may still have a social life, but it consists more and more of fellow-waifs, with fewer of the ambitious and eligible young men, who are busy chasing even younger secretaries.

What is particularly bitter about spinsterhood in the office is that it provides no compensations. Still doing the job at forty that she was doing at twenty, her life is maddeningly static. She has not had the increments of money, position, and dignity that sweeten the ageing process for the men she started out with. She may no longer share a flat, but she certainly doesn't have a house. She may be given her own office, but that is more to get her away from everyone else than to reward her. A girl of twenty could do her job better, and quite frankly they wish she'd go and make room for such a girl.

Many women have tried to prolong their period of youth and gaiety, and to extend their years of "fun." But they are treading a knife-edge—if they have a career to keep them interesting, and to substitute for their fading sex appeal, they might just make it for a while; but if they try to keep on just for the sake of the social life, and use the job as nothing more than an inconvenient necessity, they are doomed. They will be less fun than the inevitably younger girls, as well as less fun than the more successful girls. If they don't end up married, they have had it.

Many girls are forced to change jobs to prolong the fun years; in fact, it's one of the things that keeps the turnover rate up. It's not so much that in any one office they expect to meet the ideal man; few girls are that naïve, and they don't really expect to marry anyone they discover at work. The real reason for the job-change is to prevent themselves from being written off as a girl who has been around too long. It is damaging to have the people at work, who for most city girls form the main source of outside introductions and social life, thinking of you as a has-been. If you fail to succeed with one man introduced by your office colleagues, they may well decide that you are a failure and stop trying. Your chances of job progression fade as the company begins to associate you with the niche they've put you in. The routine threatens to submerge you completely. A fresh start might just manage to make you seem fresh again, or at least not quite so used as you're beginning to feel.

So the sexy-secretary image keeps women on the move in their efforts to live up to it, and it penalizes those who try to progress, or even stay in the same place, in one office. It also provides a rich source of fantasy-life for everyone in the office, which undoubtedly helps them to bear the tedium.

Young girls at their typewriters are notoriously engrossed in sexual daydreams. The men in offices fantasize too, but the great age for the daydream is adolescence. Adolescent boys are just as obsessed as girls, but they are not thrown back on their fantasies to occupy their minds in quite the same way as the girls. They are likely to be a bit more mobile—if they are not still in school, they are in first jobs as messenger boys, drivers, trainees, or apprentices, or they are in the army. Their days have a faster pace and more variety, and may even include some actual sex.

If a girl at her first typing job didn't have her daydreams, she would go out of her mind. In fact she is quite literally out of her mind for most of the day. She far prefers the routine tasks that need no attention from her consciousness; she may save up all the difficult problems and try to get them all out of the way first thing in the morning, or just before lunch. The dozy afternoons are devoted to dream scenarios—with Jean-Paul Belmondo on the Riviera, or with James Bond in the Alps. Sometimes the dreams have a Walter Mitty element—she sees herself on the stage of a night club, before an audience of attractive men pulsating with desire. She is the only woman at the presidential press conference, or (somehow) the only one in the space capsule.

These dreams turn imperceptibly into fantasies about clothes, self-improvement, suddenly looking completely different. The closest they come to touching reality is when she thinks, "What would I be wearing if . . . ?" She then plans to save up for an outfit in which she can see herself doing something not too different from the girl in her dreams.

Although the dreams may take a practical turn, they are almost never about the little house and babies that male mythology places in the dreams of young girls. This may be what they really "want," but they don't want it in the delicious, agonized, hopeless way they want their dreams of action, romance, and beauty. They are dreaming of freedom, not of its opposite.

The air of sexual excitement that young girls give to the office comes, in an oblique way, from these daydreams. Whether or not the hero of them actually works there, or whether the girl's dreams include the office in any way at all (usually they don't), she has an air of expectation and hope that keeps her incredibly responsive and attractive through months or years of dreary tasks. Erik Erikson notices this in the essay for which he has been vilified by Women's Liberation, "Reflections on Womanhood."

> The singular loveliness and brilliance which young women display in an array of activities obviously removed from the future function of childbearing is one of those esthetic experiences (for herself and for others) which almost seem to transcend all goals and purposes and therefore come to symbolize the self-containment of pure being—wherefore

young women, in the arts of the ages, have served as the visible representation of ideals and ideas, and as the creative man's muse, anima, and enigma. . . . But a true moratorium must have a term and a conclusion: womanhood arrives when attractiveness and experience have succeeded in selecting what is to be admitted to the custody of the inner space "for keeps."[21]

The typist's daydreams keep this quality alive in her for a while, but they connect neither with her "future function of childbearing" nor with any function she can plausibly connect with her working life. There is no way to translate her dreams into reality. It is usually said that the unrealistic romanticism of youth has to give way before the realities of adult life; for such a girl, it is not so much a question of sorting out the possible from the impossible in her fantasies as of abandoning this whole part of her experience or at least relegating it to an infrequently visited corner of her mind.

As this process takes place, her glow leaves her, and she is unwilling to give the job anything more than its absolute requirements. She is bored by office flirtations, sees through the feeble morale-raising efforts of management, is hostile to eager young newcomers. In this frame of mind, marriage and continuing work are almost equally unattractive alternatives—but the first is at least new.

There are perhaps deeper reasons for the introduction of carefully managed sex into the office in the guise of secretaries. Marcuse sees it as part of the large-scale manipulation of the modern corporate employee:

Without ceasing to be an instrument of labor, the body is allowed to exhibit its sexual features in the everyday work world and in work relations. This is one of the unique achievements of industrial society—rendered possible by the reduction of dirty and heavy physical labor; by the availability of cheap, attractive clothing, beauty culture, and physical hygiene; by the requirements of the advertising industry, etc. The sexy office and sales girls, the handsome, virile junior executive and floorwalker are highly marketable commodities, and the possession of suitable mistresses— once the prerogative of kings, princes, and lords—facilitates the career of even the less exalted ranks in the business community. . . . But no matter how controlled the mobilization of instinctual energy may be (it sometimes amounts to a scientific management of libido), no matter how much it may serve as a prop for the status quo—it is also gratifying to the managed individuals, just as racing the outboard motor, pushing the power lawn mower, and speeding the automobile are fun. . . .

The range of socially permissible and desirable satisfaction is greatly enlarged, but through this satisfaction, the Pleasure Principle is reduced—deprived of the claims which are irreconcilable with the established society. Pleasure, thus adjusted, generates submission.[22]

If anyone doubts that sex is being consciously manipulated by the company, what other explanation does he have for the selective awarding of secretaries? For the careful hiring of attractive girls, and the penalties visited upon executives who are so attracted by them that they leave their families? For the extraordinary admonitions to the girls: they must raise their skirts high enough to be chic, but not high enough to be too provocative. Sex in the office is another way to bind people to their work, and it is carefully cleansed of too disturbing elements before it is let in the office door.

This is certainly one explanation for the office's insistence on the traditional role of women, and its hostility to job equality. The excuses that men "won't" work for a woman, and that men "don't like" pushy lady executives sound phony: when were employees ever so carefully consulted about what they did and didn't like? Why should they be pandered to on this issue? But sex is being managed as an important part of their contentment at work, and it is far easier to keep it that way than to satisfy the workers in other ways—with money, job satisfaction, or real power. The secretary is more gratifying than a company car, and not much more expensive.

Finally, the sexy-secretary myth is used to manipulate the girls themselves. The "wouldn't you rather be desired than equal?" line, in disguised form, is behind all the injunctions to flatter, wheedle, and support the boss. It is implied that love is the reward, and that it is infinitely more worth having than anything else she could possibly dream of. This is the office version of the usual female con, and it has an added element of subtlety—the implication that she is more desirable, because free, unattainable, and self-supporting, than the wife. She has the best of both worlds—what more does she want?

The secretary feels herself to be free because she is not rewarded solely for her sex or for her work. Although her attractiveness is short-lived and precarious, it is easy to reap the rewards of it while it lasts. It is certainly far easier than anything else she can think of.

Chapter Four
THE MAKING OF A SECRETARY

THE "REAL" SECRETARY, the prototype of the advertisements and jokes, every man's dream and every girl's ambition, is well in the minority in most offices. She is only typical in the sense that she gives the office its characteristic tone and sets the behavior pattern for the typists, machine operators, switchboard girls, and file clerks who outnumber her. She is also a target of aspiration. As Germaine Greer says, "A switchboard-secretary-receptionist is a utility model: the private secretary is custom-built racing style."[1]

Few generalizations can be made about office women. In America alone, there are seven and a half million of them. Office work is the largest single female occupation, and in terms of class and education, it attracts more than its share of people who represent the national average. Three-fifths of female high-school graduates go into the office. Of the college graduates who don't become teachers, about 10 per cent become secretarial and clerical workers. The proportion of secretaries decreases gradually among richer and better-educated women, and it also drops off at the other end of the scale. The girl who drops out of high school has a slightly better chance of entering the office than she used to have, but she is still far more likely to do manual work.[2]

In Britain, female office workers seem to come almost equally from the lower middle class and the upper working class. The same proportion of female university graduates go into the office as in the United States, but they are a far smaller percentage of their age group.

Within this vast cross-section of the female population, there are many distinct gradations of social class, which are translated into distinctions at work. It is often assumed that an office girl slowly progresses from the typing pool to the carpeted office of the "executive secretary." But in fact few girls seem to make much progress once they enter the office. It reflects enduring social distinctions as faithfully as does the school system. Although the intelligent and ambitious can use the opportunities provided by school, or by the office, to climb the class ladder, both serve on the whole to perpetuate the status quo.

The typist aged seventeen may get out of the pool, be assigned to a small group of men, and begin calling herself a secretary, but she will probably never be a personal assistant to an important executive. The girl who runs the managing director's office, with her cool poise and expensive accent, probably spent a year or two as a junior stenographer before landing her plum job, but she was destined for it from the start. The process of selection goes back as far as birth, and is reinforced by the prestige gradations of secretarial schools. The schoolgirl seeking her first job may get some help from a school guidance counsellor, but she is more likely to pick up shorthand and typing in a summer course at a large commercial school and then throw herself on the mercy of one of the large agencies.

The select secretary, on the other hand, may spend up to a year at a secretarial school that has some of the aspects of a finishing school—even if she doesn't learn French provincial cooking or "grooming and poise," she will learn one of the old-fashioned, difficult symbol shorthands, some business accounting and office procedure, and perhaps a language. Her job will be selected from the hundreds begging for graduates of the school, or perhaps it will be passed on to her by a friend or a previous graduate who is leaving it.

There is one way in which the true secretary can be picked out from the mass of office girls—she describes herself, proudly, as a secretary. The ambitious girl, usually with a degree, who is anxious to use her secretarial job as a springboard to something else will avoid using the word as much as possible. If she can get away with it, she will call herself an assistant. If she isn't questioned too closely, she can imply all sorts of things with an airy, "I work for C.B.S." On the other hand, she may exaggerate the lowliness of her condition—"I'm just working as a typist"—with the implication that the job is a temporary embarrassment, and that her real vocation, soon to be realized, lies elsewhere.

The file girl, or the inhabitant of the vast typing pool or computer room, can be equally vague about her job and give an equal impression of indifference to it. "Oh, I work in an office," or "I work for a bank," can imply, "Let's talk about something else—how can this possibly be interesting?"

Neither of these girls usually get to top-secretary jobs, which require considerable commitment. Discontent and alienation in any form are quickly spotted in the office, and they disqualify a potential secretary faster than anything else. Thus, the true secretary begins with a favorable attitude towards the job and its title, and the girls with this attitude form a fairly homogeneous group within the vast office staff.

The secretary proper has gravitated towards her job in somewhat the same way as the man she works for has come to his. Broad social divisions and their effect on career choices work for women as well as for men; although the executive's secretary may be less committed to her job than the executive is to his, there are reasons why they are both in that company rather than any other, and these reasons give a clue to many of their shared attitudes.

The secretary who goes into business is likely to share many of the "typical businessman" attitudes of her boss, on everything from the iniquity of unions to the traditional role of women to the evils of communism. The more intellectual girl who goes into publishing or journalism is equally likely to share her boss's views on the supreme worth of creative achievement, the necessity for social revolution, and the rapacity of big business. But while these views feed her discontent with her ancillary, traditional, docile role, the prevailing ideology of the business corporation is likely to reconcile the secretary there to her lot.

An important part of the business creed is the value it attaches to the executive, whose high salary is regarded as the result of fierce bidding for scarce talent. What he does can be difficult to define, as we have seen: some ideologists of business compare him to the manager of a baseball team, while others content themselves with phrases about "decision-making." But the more mysterious his function, in contrast to the mechanical functions of "experts," the more awe-inspiring his successes.

The executive's hegemony over his employees is one part of the business system that has scarcely been questioned at all. It is his business to run the company profitably, and if the workers don't like it they can leave. This view has been challenged by industrial workers, but the office still largely shares the management's view and identifies itself with the owners. The executive's secretary, especially, is imbued with his interests and does not question his values. Her self-esteem is based on her valuation of him: the more important he is, the more worthwhile is her service.

The individualism and self-reliance preached by the business creed might be expected to rub off on the secretary, but here her sex comes into play.

> The home, when it is mentioned at all, is generally treated as an ultimate value which may be threatened by unsound developments and which must be protected against any such threats. While the businessman may in fact have had to leave his parental home in search of opportunity, protect his business rationality against the claims of relatives, or struggle bitterly to balance the claims of office and family on his time and energies, little or no call for "progressive" evolution of our kinship system appears in the ideology. The tone is eminently conservative, stressing traditional duties.[3]

The traditional duties of woman are to serve man, take her status from him, and (these days) to combine work and home in such a way as to give him optimum service without competition. If this is the creed of the secretary's boss, it is not surprising that she not only believes it, but lives it.

Belief in this creed has not often been widespread among those who did not stand to benefit from it. Marxist accusations of "false consciousness," particularly among the lower middle classes, merely indicate that this group has considered that its interest lies in making the best of an existing situation, rather than in trying to change it by revolutionary means. The secretaries seem to Women's Liberationists incredibly unaware of their own interests, but they do stand to make some gains from their social conservatism. First of all, their jobs are near the top of the female scale. A few professional women may surpass them, but they will in turn do better than many of the alienated girls with high ambitions who are frustrated by the system. Similarly, although they may not interest the most prestigious men, who are secure enough to want their prestige enhanced by women of high achievement, most businessmen will prefer them to the girls who reject the conservative creed.

There are, however, indications of alienation even among the most conformist of secretaries. They job-hop and malinger early in their careers; they escape work through daydreams, gossip, and trivialities; they husband-hunt relentlessly enough to give rise to the suspicion that they are longing to leave the job altogether. But whatever their dissatisfactions, their background gives them no real mechanism for expressing discontent. They may feel guilty about it, and they usually blame themselves for not making the most of the job, staying in school longer, or being talented enough to impress their superiors.

The usual form in which questionnaires (the sort put out by employment agencies or large companies) try to get at such a secretary's feelings on the "woman question" is to ask her in one way or another, whether she wouldn't rather have her boss's job than her own. But what does this mean? A cardinal article of the conservative faith is that talent is rewarded by the system; if she is not very well rewarded, she must not have much talent. Why would the firm want to keep her down on purpose? What's more, if her boss doesn't deserve his spectacular salary, what is she doing working for him? The firm surely wouldn't give him a secretary if his time weren't valuable.

The secretary's whole world-view is geared to these propositions. She has had little contact with the trade-union questioning of the system on the one hand, or with the intellectuals' questioning of it on the other. All her conditioning has taught her that "adjustment" to the system is the mark of a healthy, cooperative, normal person, and that the critics of "free enterprise" are probably sick, if not actually subversive.

In America, this sort of conditioning is the function of the public high school, the classic and most prolific source of secretaries. Indeed, the high school is now under severe attack from the same people who are attacking the traditional female role, and for much the same reasons. They charge that both institutions inculcate obedience, docility, and conformity at the expense of originality and independence. And they have shown that high school embodies the most conservative aspects of American society.

Certainly high school could scarcely be better suited to the production of secretaries. The school imposes office-like routines on its students: they must be there for a certain number of hours, with valid excuses for any absence. Compliance with routine is crucial: neat papers delivered on time, forms filled out correctly, everything accounted for, often seem to be the real goals of the system—what is actually contained in the papers is more or less irrelevant.

The status quo is respected by both the school and the office: free enterprise and the dangers of communism are preached by both. Sexual roles are clearly defined—in most high schools, girls learn sewing and typing while boys take metal shop and play football. Neatness in appearance is prized, and great controversies rage over hair length, skirt length, and girls in trousers.

Girls usually behave better and perform better in high school. They are docile, obedient, and do their homework and sit still in class. Boys have a harder time, since the school's aims conflict with what they are told—both before and after they enter school—are the male characteristics. The aggression, restlessness, independence that are encouraged both in the small boy and in the businessman contrast with the high-school frame of mind, and make it difficult for boys to adapt to it.

High school tends to channel boys in two directions—into college or into a "vocation," or manual trade. It is not very well suited to preparing them for either one. It does not encourage intellectualism, which is likely to present a challenge to the prevailing conformist ideology, known as "equality" or "democracy" in high school. Nor does it really respect manual work; the attention paid to it is slighting and puts it on a level with optional basketball. It is used as a punishment for failure in the "hard" academic subjects. So the boys are likely to be alienated from the high-school scene from the start.

But the girls are no problem at all. All they need in the way of manual training is a little typing, and possibly some shorthand; and these can just as well be provided later on by a secretarial school. The level of English taught in high school is almost precisely what is needed by an office girl, and the level of general knowledge is appropriate too. The behavior required is exactly similar—a girl who has spent four years sitting in class with a notebook on her knee doesn't even have to change her posture as she moves to the office.

From the first, high school was designed to educate girls to a useful level and not beyond: they were first admitted because primary school teachers were needed in large numbers, and even those who didn't believe in educating women saw that it order to use them as a source of cheap labor, they would have to allow them to be trained. High-school education was also demanded by the first employers of women in offices—it had none of the drawbacks of college, which was likely to fill a girl's head with notions.

In many offices nowadays, entrance requirements have gone up to include some college; but this has happened just as the expansion of higher education has made many colleges more like high schools. The required level of competence has not changed; what has changed is the high school's ability to provide it. *The Organization Man,* published in 1956, showed that business and other "practical" courses were replacing the humanities and sciences as the basis of the college curriculum. "Business English" has replaced the study of literature; "mental hygiene" that of psychology. Colleges have been attempting ever more strenuously to prepare their students for the organization life.

This process has filtered right down through the school system. A parent in the suburb studied by Whyte said, "Janet is studying marketing, and she's only in the sixth grade. She's studying ads and discounts—things I didn't get until college. These kids are certainly getting a broad view of things."[4]

What neither Whyte nor anyone else foresaw was the resistance this socializing process would encounter during the sixties. Not only did Sputnik start a wave of criticism of "life adjustment" courses among educators themselves, but the strains placed on American society by racism, Vietnam, and deterioration of the environment were reflected in students' refusal to be prepared for life in such a society.

Most of the rebellion took place on the college campuses, but it has also been directed against the high schools. It has come from two sides.

First, the "blackboard jungle" type of rebellion was sparked off by the inability of the high schools to do the task they set themselves—to socialize all youth, no matter how black or deprived, into the middle class. Inner-city high schools have just about given up on this task, and most now admit that they are no more than baby-sitting devices or jails. The young to whom a promise has been held out and then withdrawn are angry, and their white middle-class teachers often seem to them to be the symbol of the system's mockery.

Even were the schools to succeed, they would provide no guarantee of entry into the office world, whose conformity is even more resistant to change than that of the schools.

The attack has come from another quarter, too. The big, affluent suburban high schools are in the throes of a rebellion that echoes the turmoil of college students. And this is no accident—the cause of the rebellion is the clash between the "college" attitudes the kids have absorbed from parents, older brothers and sisters, and books, and the high-school reality they are forced into. From their sophisticated point of view, the high school is channeling them towards a life they have already rejected.

Both these attacks portray the high school as the main avenue into office life, and the offices would agree. They are on the watch for the same symbols that the school tries to stamp out— long hair and all the rest of it. But it is hard not to believe that the attack on the high schools will go further towards changing the office than will any change of heart on the part of people already there. Today's secretaries may have already been crushed by the system; but tomorrow's will be on the alert when the process begins.

The "secondary modern schools" in Britain, now being turned, with the "grammar schools," into "comprehensives," have attempted to follow the egalitarian pattern of American education. One of the consequences of this policy has been the attempt to train girls for secretarial jobs, and this process is in some ways more overt and far-reaching than it has been in the United States. The ideology of class is still stronger in Britain than in America, and this has affected the aspirations of most children, who do not dream of professional status, suburban houses, or entrepreneurial fortunes nearly as readily as their American counterparts.

A *New Statesman* reporter visiting a girls' school talked to a class of thirty-two girls. Twenty-eight wanted to be secretaries, and four wanted to be hairdressers. Secretarial training is so practical and so easily obtainable that to the graduating student it puts all other prospects in the shade. For the minimally trained teenager, the salaries are unbelievably enticing; and the advertising of the large agencies adds the final seductive note.

But mass secretarial training in the schools has been a dismal failure. In fact, it bears out the suspicions of such anti-school polemicists as Ivan Illich, who claims that incarceration in school is the best way *not* to teach something, and that skills found to be necessary will be quickly and easily learned by any adult.

The London *Times* of July 17, 1970 reports, "There have been attempts to equip all schoolgirl leavers with secretarial skills, but ... it was found they were counterproductive. A short dose of shorthand each week was the surest way of killing interest and destroying confidence." There are still widespread attempts to teach typing in schools, and it has been found that the primary years are the best time to learn it. But the whole exercise would seem less like a sinister attempt to slot people into their appointed places in the job structure if the instruction were given to boys too. Whatever its short-term advantages, a plan to turn all schoolgirls into secretaries sounds like social engineering of the most Orwellian kind.

It is strange to see how the school system's attempts at egalitarianism, particularly in America, have imposed on girls a role that is so patently "unequal." The secretary is Miss Average, and thus Miss Democracy. The rules of the system penalize the "different." "Cute" looks and lots of "personality" are more important than any really distinctive attributes. Perhaps this is true of all adolescence, but it seems to have reached its zenith in the creation of the high-school girl, cheerleader and baby-sitter, and in her transformation into the secretary.

Anyone who criticizes this ideal is positively un-American, usually either a communist or an effete snob or both. Even in a film showing a man marrying a secretary, the old-fashioned idea that he might have married beneath him is introduced only to be ridiculed. It is a device for showing the ridiculous snobbery of the upper classes; real class differences on which such snobbery might base itself are minimized. In *Stranger in My Arms* (1959), a society boy marries a secretary despite the objections of his mother. The secretary turns out to be a true-blue girl any man would be proud to have, while the mother is corrupt, vicious, and thinks that money can buy anything.

But the movies have usually found the secretary just a little too acceptable to be dramatic. A plot can be built up around a career girl: Should she put her work before the man she loves? Can she make a man happy? Can she get the man away from his wife? Are mink and diamonds any compensation for the lack of a home and children? But the only romantic plot imaginable around a secretary is will she or won't she sleep with her boss, and the dramatic possibilities of that one are easily exhausted.

The movies and television, however, are still full of secretaries, even if they are not the leading ladies. There are plenty of glamorous offices filled with glamorous girls, usually about as far removed from reality as the Doris Day comedies are from real split-level life. The secretary sits there responding instantly to the frantic "Miss Smith, get me the governor"; the detective who is on the track of her boss, or the traitor who is gunning for his job, sits on the edge of her desk and flirts for a minute while waiting for admission to the sanctum.

She sometimes helps things along by a white lie to the boss's wife or a tip about his temper to a subordinate who is about to launch an ill-timed scheme. In the James Bond novels, she helps him out in all sorts of unobtrusive ways, dreams and worries about him when he's gone, has the good sense to keep this happy scene going by never giving in to him, and is amply rewarded for it all by an occasional postcard from the battlefront. And while the sexy heroines meet grisly deaths or simply disappear between one book and the next, Miss Moneypenny goes on forever.

Although secretaries come from all strata, in the media they are always the same, vaguely lower middle class. They are the social inferiors of their bosses, but not by very much, so that while it would be inappropriate—unless a special point about "democracy" is being made—for the boss to marry the secretary, he can perfectly acceptably have a drink with her and tell her his problems. He knows that there will be nothing more interesting in her life than himself and his concerns, and that he is richer and more glamorous than her own father, boyfriends, and neighbors. She knows, when seated in a mid-town bar with her boss, that this is the nearest she will ever get to the high life. She accepts the prospect of a suburban or small-town existence forever afterwards, but these moments of glamor are to her what his years at Yale are to a Midwestern businessman—something to remember and be slightly nostalgic about; contact with a bigger world.

Historically, the Cinderella theme was the basis for most of the stories about secretaries that began to appear when publishers realized that working girls were a new mass audience. They simply took over the existing formula: instead of the governess marrying the titled employer, the penniless stenographer won the heart of the boss's son.

The novelty of unchaperoned contact between the sexes was the basis for these stories, which were always highly moralistic. The media to this day have needed to believe that the secretaries were "good" girls; the idea that they might not be is flirted with only to make way for the triumphant affirmation at the end.

Moral precepts play a big part in what is by far the largest category of literature aimed at secretaries, the advice manuals.

For at least two generations after the first secretaries went to work, the nation, for obscure reasons of its own, preferred to pretend that sex had nothing to do with the sensational popularity of female typewriter operators. All sorts of explanations were offered: women were said to have a peculiar aptitude for work requiring finger dexterity, and to be more conscientious than men, and better custodians of confidential business secrets. Thousands of words—pamphlets, books and magazine articles—were written about the path to success as a secretary. Almost without exception the authors recommended modesty in dress and manners; taste and neatness, but no flash. In the early fiction written with secretaries for heroines, the hero (a rising young executive in the firm) was usually so impressed by his secretary's decorum that he didn't dare even to propose; in one story after another he called her in and dictated a proposal, building to the climax in which she, her eyes brimming with tears, asked, "And to whom, sir, is this missive to be addressed?"[5]

In the manuals, such exciting possibilities are not even hinted at. An occasional warning about attempting to mix friendship with business, or an assertion that a too friendly boss is the cue to begin job-hunting, are the only mentions of office sex.

The primness of the manuals is often the reflection of an attempt to protect girls from being exploited in the big, tough city. Like worried mothers, the authors try to warn against advances from married men, unwanted attentions from coworkers, and other perils. Safety first is the idea, and behind it is the assumption that a girl can impair her marriageability by not protecting herself against the office predators. To avoid any possible misunderstanding, she must be as drab as a governess. The double standard, according to the manuals, is still enshrined in the minds of most men, and the long-term rewards of respectability are greater than the illusory attentions gained by obvious sexuality.

In fact, the more self-effacing the secretary can manage to be, the better. This sometimes reaches an almost masochistic level. One article aimed at secretaries suggests that their handbags should contain anything the boss might need—clothes brush, black thread, Alka-Seltzer, etc. One suggests that the secretary can keep the boss on good terms with his wife by putting on the calendar a series of reminders—flowers, gifts, birthdays, anniversaries—and seeing that the things are delivered with appropriate cards. Most say that the boss should be shielded from the consequences of his own mistakes and that the secretary must take the blame. A few go so far as to suggest that she should even pretend to *him* that it was her fault, since his ego is more important than his grasp of the truth.

All the books are stuffed with advice on what the secretary needs to know, most of it on a level that any competent city-dweller would have reached anyway. They don't quite tell her how to look things up in the phone book, but they do go into details like "How to make a long-distance call," "How to find out the postal charges to different countries," "Some common abbreviations." The theoretical level is dealt with by a few banalities about tact, poise, grooming, and the like.

Even these books, with their insistence that secretarial work is a satisfying, even exciting life for a girl, fail to make it remotely interesting. There is no disguising the tedium of the rituals they describe. I can imagine no better way of discouraging potential secretaries than by making them read the advice books—it's almost as good as talking to a few twenty-year veterans.

The Pollyanna tone of some of the secretarial manuals is almost too much to believe. One says, on the subject of the "foot in the door."

> Office work may exert such a powerful hold on us that it diverts us from an intended career in another field. This is likely to happen when a girl takes an office job for the purpose of saving up for training in one of the professions. After a year or two she finds office work a fascinating career in itself.[6]

The same book asserts, "It is fortunate that most bosses are men. For just as women prefer men bosses, the men prefer women for office jobs."[7]

Its description of the office is resolutely complacent, and makes a virtue of the conformity and mediocrity that often characterize office style. "Our speech is neither the slang of the factory nor the vocabulary of the college professor. It is straightforward and to the point—the language of business."[8]

It claims that a college degree will sometimes help a girl land a job, but that in the long run it is not such a good thing, as it will make her dissatisfied. It asserts that of New York personnel directors looking for female office staff, 38 per cent prefer a high-school graduate and only 26 per cent prefer a college graduate. How it reconciles this finding with its idea that office work is a satisfying alternative to a professional career remains a mystery.

The secretarial manuals often talk about the secretary's job in the terms women's magazines use for that of the wife. One describes the secretary as "partner-typist-waitress-valet-filing-clerk-hostess-accountant-nurse,"[9] in a list reminiscent of those (directed at wives) so beloved of *Ladies' Home Journal* writers ("chauffeur-cook-hostess-decorator-accountant-mistress," etc., etc.).

The same book explores the secretary's role in the office in terms that also relate it to the traditional male-female roles.

> Of course, if, after your careful cogitation and your explanation of the problem and your proposed solution, he then solemnly decides on a solution *which is precisely the one which you have given him*—well, you will learn to accept it with a poker-face as *his* suggestion. Men are like that![10]

This book, too, adopts an "all is for the best in the best of all possible worlds" tone.

> You have to look this matter squarely in the face and ask yourself: "Am I personally discriminated against, or does my company in general, differentiate between men and women?" In the majority of instances, you will find the problem is not personal.[11]
> Whenever you cooperate with a superior, you risk being accused of trying to "take over." In this respect, women have the advantage over men. They do not compete for their boss's job. This allows them freedom of action.[12]

The whims and prejudices of the boss are looked on as part of the job, not to be worried about or taken personally, but just some of the facts of life that have to be lived with. One executive is described who couldn't stand turban hats, and would not have a secretary who wore one. "Such cases are not unusual. A rubber company executive refuses to hire girls under five feet, eight inches tall. A newspaper representative insists on redheads."[13]

Age is, of course, a problem because it arouses all of our whimsical executive's fears and prejudices.

> Women who aren't fashionable become a problem to their boss. He may appreciate their good work. But he doesn't like it if other executives ridicule his department as being "full of fuddy-duddies." He may have worked with these women over a period of years. Instinctively he feels he is in the same age group as they are and this makes him seem older himself.[14]

Finally, the same advise is dished out to office girls as is given to girls who want to be popular in high school.

> Don't let your brains show too much. A woman was offered a job as a typist. During the interview, the man who was hiring her mentioned that he was taking a course in a nearby college. She was on the verge of divulging that she had taken this course herself, and could help him with the homework. She wisely kept still.[15]

As is the case for the "organization man," brains in the secretary are looked on in these books not as assets to the organization, but as pure showing off, likely to create bad feeling in the group.

The office's demands for conformity are looked on as reasonable and necessary, although of course they all work one way—the secretary can be fired for old age or bad breath, but she must put up with the boss's appearance and mannerisms, no matter how disgusting.

The National Secretaries Association's manual, *Secretaries on the Spot* (1961), tackles such "discussion" questions as "When does a person need tactful 'correction' on dress, odor, overweight, etc.? When will she regretfully have to be fired?"

This book has something of the tone of textbooks for high-school "family living" or "adjustment" courses. The way popularizers of psychology asserted that a woman who attempted to do something outside the traditional female role needed counseling to help her "accept her femininity," those who don't fit in at the office must either be corrected or got rid of.

The "life adjustment" movement in American education was designed to give to every student the sort of knowledge that would be useful to him in the life he was likely to lead—for most students, the argument ran, this was not

> to fit them to become a disciplined part of the world of production and competition, ambition and vocation, creativity, and analytical thought, but rather to help them learn the ways of the world of consumption and hobbies, of enjoyment and social complaisance—in short, to adapt gracefully to the passive and hedonistic style summed up in the significant term *adjustment*.[16]

One New York State course in "Home and Family Living" covered such topics as

> "Developing school spirit," "My duties as a baby sitter," "Clicking with the crowd," "How to be liked," "What can be done about acne?" "Learning to care for my bedroom," "Making my room more attractive." Eighth-grade pupils were given these questions on a true-false test: "Just girls need to use deodorants." "Cake soap can be used for shampooing."[17]

"Adjustment" in the office revolves around such questions, discussed in *Secretaries on the Spot*, as "First woman in all-male office: Was this girl foolhardy to tackle such a job?" and "Are college girls at a disadvantage in fitting in with a predominantly non-college group?" Even more sinister is the example given under the heading "Older Worker Becomes Inefficient":

> A secretary had a serious talk with the "older" woman one morning before any other employees arrived concerning her

health and retirement plans. She realized she was not eligible for a pension and gratefully accepted the lump-sum settlement management had arranged. A party in her honor was planned where she received a gold watch from the company and smaller gifts from other employees. She received state compensation for seven months and then with the help of friends obtained a position in a trust company to work in a clerical capacity. She will soon be eligible for social-security benefits to supplement her income.[18]

Once a girl has "adjusted" herself out of ambition, adjusted herself out of competitiveness, adjusted herself out of anything but the most mindless obedience, she gets adjusted right out of the company to which she has so desperately conformed, and adjusts herself into accepting its utter indifference to her fate. And the company is never wrong—a secretary who questions it can be replaced before she knows what's happening.

While Mrs. Smith might get away for a while with being unfriendly to her husband's customers, his secretary won't get away with it at all. Divorces cost money and take time, but firing a secretary takes less than five minutes—and doesn't cost a penny![19]

This gleeful observation provides a clue to much of the reasoning behind the build-up of the secretary mystique. The intimacy and close dependence of the boss-secretary relationship are stressed (the comparison with "Mrs. Smith") to emphasize the unreasonableness of expecting even ordinary work mores to apply. An ordinary worker might be justified in claiming that it was unfair to fire him for such purely personal reasons, but the secretary, because of her special emotional role, is exempt from the usual safeguards.

All these descriptions of the secretary are set in the context of a fairly large business corporation, and this is where most of the breed are to be found. Other sorts of secretarial employers—universities, governments, individuals—create other atmospheres and make other demands. But the typical businessman's secretary is expected to enhance his status as a tycoon, and what she likes about working for him is exactly this atmosphere of tycoonery.

Instead of dreaming of "marrying up" the power scale, the businessman's secretary dreams of "working up." The more prestigious her boss, the more exciting he is to be around. The more demanding and impossible he is, the better his secretary likes it. The big entrepreneur, or important celebrity, noted for his ruthlessness and brutality to his employees, is her ideal:

> This combination of egotism, vanity, selfishness, desire for recognition and speed at taking offence are not, of course, the most engaging characteristics. ... And yet these people very often, almost always, collect a devoted group of people around them. One reason for this is their very strong, personal magnetism; another is that they provide an objective, a purpose, the task of building something, which most people find attractive and many irresistible. ... "He for God only, she for God in him": Milton's expression of the relationship between Adam and Eve is often true of the leader and his group.[20]

David Frost's secretary boasts of the time he dictated nonstop across the Atlantic; an advertising girl recalls tracking down three elephants in half an hour for a commercial. Others nostalgically remember whirlwind trips to deliver important papers, reports typed overnight before big meetings, or simply the day-to-day effort of living up to a demanding job without ever admitting ignorance or inability to cope.

Part of the pleasure of this kind of job is the lack of routine; part is the feeling of being connected, however distantly, with the kind of great events that are reported in the newspapers. But much of it is the excitement of being in the company of a man who frequents the clubs and board rooms that would never admit his secretary.

The high-powered secretary is herself sometimes admitted to enclaves where no woman has been before. And she is not necessarily the invisible helper behind the scenes—as the only woman present, she can be the focus of considerable interest and gallantry. This is enhanced by the fact that she has arrived without threatening or competing with the men, or otherwise stepping out of her feminine role. The men are glad to have her there. She presents them with no dilemmas about how to treat her, none of the nervousness that often greets the executive woman—"Will she be offended if I ask her to take minutes?" "Should her husband be invited to parties where we bring our wives?"

The women who work for politicians feel just as special and just as close to the center of the action. The feeling of being an "insider" is very important to them, and they are as fascinated by political gossip as are their bosses. The memoirs of Ainsley Gotto, the secretary who was accused of toppling Australian Prime Minister John Gorton (his opponents used her constant presence as the basis for a smear campaign), are full of descriptions of White House dinners, parties with the Kennedys and their "boiler-room girls," and thumbnail sketches of the famous— a far cry from most girls' memories of their working lives.

It has been observed[21] that the only two modern statesmen who risked their careers for love were Franklin Roosevelt and Lloyd George. The former fell in love with his wife's social secretary, the latter with his children's governess, whom he made his secretary as a way of keeping her around without arousing comment. In both cases, the man in the all-male world at the top saw very few women in the ordinary course of his life, so the ones who had a natural excuse for proximity to him had a distinct advantage.

Political secretaries are often awed by their bosses, and highly protective of them. They get furious with the wives, who don't seem to understand the great man's need for deference and privacy. Someday, they fantasize, he will look up from his desk and say, "Don't think I haven't noticed your devotion, your sacrifices...." In the meantime, the secretary makes do with brief smiles as the orders are rapped out. She may be the only person who believes the rhetoric handed out by the publicity office about her boss—that he's serving a noble aim, his idealism and integrity are absolute, his electoral appeal is boundless.

Show-biz secretaries are an altogether more disillusioned breed. They feel comfortably superior to the wives, actresses, models, and society girls who compete for the sexual attention of their bosses. The secretaries know that they are likely to be around longer than any of the others because they are reliable; they do everything from delivering the kids to boarding school to decorating the houses; they know everyone in the business. What does the latest wife know about her husband's record contract? Can his girlfriend even make a decent cup of coffee?

These girls are contemptuously disapproving of the vulgarity, the open exploitation, the violent sexuality of the life surrounding the film business. They all have a story to tell about leaving a job when asked to undress or take dictation in the bath or clean up after a wild party. They love to see through the common illusions about the glamorous private lives of the stars—"Him! I could tell you a thing or two about him!"

Yet such girls embody the Western world's ambivalence towards its synthetic idols. They are attracted, even glamorized, by the Disneyland world of television-promoted celebrities, packaged entertainment, and armchair "adventure." Like the stewardesses, their ideas of a desirable life are formed by the very media they so hotly denounce.

In the entourages of the rich, some of the myths about secretaries actually come true. Such men can have the choice of beautiful and skilled girls, and can make any conditions they like for giving them the job. The boss can have his "secretary" with him wherever he goes, and not have to answer to a board of directors about her pay and fringe benefits. The pickings for the girls are lucrative, and they are in the enviable position of being neither left at home with the wives, nor treated with contempt like the party girls.

Many stories—some fact, some fiction—have been told about such secretaries, who run the gamut from real "office wives," with sex merely incidental, to thinly disguised courtesans. Girls have ended up with stock portfolios, businesses of their own, or rich husbands after a few years on this circuit.

This sort of secretarial job is, however, dying out. Only the most conservative business milieu, or the political world where a show of propriety is important, needs this sort of excuse for the presence of a woman. The sexual revolution has made the whole question seem dated. Traveling businessmen are now more likely to use temporary secretaries hired on the spot; even airlines and big hotels now provide them. In fact, working for such an employer is in some ways a modern, more independent equivalent of working for one rich boss.

The homosexual twist to the secretarial game has largely died out, too. In the days of Somerset Maugham, the title of "secretary" could be used to explain the presence of a favorite boy. But it all sounds quite bizarre now, in the days of Gay Liberation.

There are still a few secretarial jobs left to excite the ambitious. Most of them are in places so exciting that any job there would be a plum. The newest and most high-powered of research institutes and magazines, the most glamorous of film companies, the offices of political insiders—all can be exciting for a while. But such a job can lead to the greatest frustration of all, because it arouses ambitions in a girl that she will probably not be able to fulfill in her own career. Even if she starts out satisfied with a secretarial job, she is not likely to be so for long. And there is no way up, for the top jobs in her company are attracting the brilliant and famous. The standards are high. From her secretarial job, she can probably move to an executive job somewhere less demanding, and trade one sort of prestige for another. But she will miss the aura of intellectual excitement she knew in her secretarial days.

The "handmaiden of the arts" secretary, who is also thrilled by her job at first, is notoriously susceptible to the same kind of disillusion. Although she is still in awe of her master, she may also become intensely jealous, sick of bringing cups of coffee to the reporters who interview *him*. She has been known to say, "It's my turn in the study," but after twenty years of fetching coffee, she has nothing left to communicate except a neurotic tirade against her oppressor. The world then remarks, "The poor man, what he must have had to put up with!"

In many ways, the secretary to the intellectual is worse off than the businessman's secretary. She may have the fun of working in an atmosphere of ideas and interesting people, but intellectual snobbery will see to it that she is accorded less respect than she would have in the corporate office. Her boss may be an "outsider" who has spent years struggling against obscurity and debt; when he finally makes it, the trappings of success become inordinately important to him, and he lords it over his secretary as few men do.

Britain's satirical magazine *Private Eye* recently commented on

> a disgraceful case of suppression of free speech at the Black Dwarf, the self-styled revolutionary organ.
>
> The Dwarf was quick to jump on the Women's Liberation bandwaggon and the issue of September 5th carried several articles on the subject, including one compiled by a group of secretaries complaining about their downtrodden lot. Two girls working for "a small group of men" protested vigorously about having to do office chores like buying lavatory paper, making coffee and in general being treated like servants in a nineteenth century middle class home.
>
> The article did not reveal that the "small group of men" who tyrannised these wretched girls in such a disgustingly bourgeois fashion were in fact the editorial committee of the New Left Review.

The intellectual has complicated justifications of his need for a secretary. Ordinarily, of course, he would disapprove of exploiting them, but in his own case, he's really so busy. . . . Sometimes he uses an economic rationale: "I don't approve of the system, but as it is, my time is simply much more valuable in money terms than hers is, and I can pay her much more than I could if I didn't use my time to the fullest advantage." He would be shocked to have it pointed out that any junior executive talks the same way. Ideologically, he is in the position of the hippie driving a Cadillac in the *New Yorker* cartoon: "As long as the system throws up these toys, we might as well play with them."

With the growth of the universities and the increasing importance to the economy of research, intellectual life has become bureaucratized. Many scholars and academics who would previously have made do with the typing services of their wives and students now run fully equipped offices, complete with secretaries. This is another opportunity for women to infiltrate the places where they have never been seen before—and to find some of the consequent frustrations.

C. Wright Mills has described this change:

> The new academic statesman, like the business executive and the military chieftain, has acquired means of competence which must be distinguished from his personal competence—but which in his reputation are not so distinguished. A permanent professional secretary, a clerk to run the library, an electric typewriter, dictating equipment, and a mimeographing machine, and perhaps a small budget of three or four thousand dollars a year for purchasing books and periodicals—even such minor office equipment and staff enormously increases any scholar's appearance of competence.[22]

England does not run to quite such lavish trappings, but the new-style academic is bringing women into even the fustiest Oxford colleges. Anthony Powell's portrait of a very worldly don includes, for the first time in the life he is describing, a secretary.

> "This is Miss Leintwardine, my—well—my secretary. That's what you are, Ada, ain't you? Sounds rather fast. All sorts of jokes about us, I'm sure. . . ."
> . . . In the role of secretary she was a little more explicable, though why on earth Sillery should require a secretary was by no means apparent. Perhaps a secretary went with being made a peer.[23]

This particular secretary uses the contacts with the male literary and academic world, which she could hardly have made in any other way, to get a fairly good job in publishing.

The female intellectuals who become successful enough to hire secretaries use them differently from men. The successful women are likely to be superefficient, very orderly, and quite demanding. They feel that any slip, any encroachment of chaos, threatens their hard-won position. Men, on the other hand, believe there is a connection between chaos and creativity, and like to have picturesquely messy studies, odd hours, disorderly clothes, and bad memories for appointments.

Thus, while the literary man's secretary must organize him as well as his work, the lady novelist likes to know that while she is being interviewed for a Sunday paper, her secretary is back in the study, transcribing the latest work at full speed.

All these categories of secretarial work tend to attract the ambitious girl who does not want to be a secretary at all. The girl who is content with the job often does not have enough prestige or intellectualism herself to please her boss, while the girl who does is likely to be irritatingly rebellious. The more highly educated girls become, the more difficult it is to find the perfect combination.

But there is one sort of secretary who is perfectly suited to this lowly niche in the high life—the sort described by columnist Jilly Cooper as Miss Nitwit-Thompson, the office deb. In the United States, she will have gone to an undemanding but classy college like Sweet Briar. In England, she is likely to be the product of a girls' public school like Roedean or Heathfield. Daddy is rich and she is perfectly happy simply to wait around until somebody equally rich marries her, but the place to wait these days is the office.

These girls have a better time at work than almost anyone else, because they can chat to the bosses on a more-than-equal basis, they can never be fired (the cachet of having them around is too great to give up), and they don't look to the office as the answer to any of their dreams, matrimonial or financial, so they are never disappointed.

They get along well with the other girls—it's almost like getting a glimpse of royalty to have them around, their clothes can be exclaimed over, and they are always very friendly in a noblesse oblige kind of way. The ambitious girls don't mind them either, because they are no threat. They change jobs quite often, leaving behind a body of admirers in each office.

These girls simply don't understand what all the fuss is about when women's rights are mentioned. It's so *earnest,* and the people involved are so dreary. As for making a career in business, this girl always knows "one very brilliant girl I was at school with" who is making a fabulous career for herself, which proves it can be done if you really want to, but "I simply don't have the brains." (The last remark is often an outright lie—she has brains enough to know what she wants and how to get it.)

There are far too few girls like this to fill all the offices that would like to have them. The man looking for unusual intelligence or social status in his secretary, who is unwilling to give more money or responsibility in return, will always have a hard time. Dreary competence will be the best he can hope for, and he will have to use different women to satisfy his different needs. Some of the roles that the businessman's secretary has managed to combine will again be separated, and the secretary may well be left with the unglamorous drudgery.

Chapter Five
THE AMBITIOUS SECRETARY

THE GIRLS WHO made office careers in the early years of the century certainly thought they were on the way to full job equality. *Kitty Foyle* and *Angel Pavement* are quite clear in their assumption that secretarial work is an apprenticeship, a stepping-stone, necessary to teach women about the hitherto mysterious business world, but by no means the end of their ambitions and capabilities.

What happened? Why are educated girls today in the same situation they were in in 1910, still patiently typing away and hoping for the big break?

The girls who ask this question with the most urgency and anguish are the college-educated, sophisticated girls who flock to the big cities—especially New York—every June, looking for a foot in the magic doors of publishing, advertising, journalism. Some of them know how tough it is going to be.

They have received two pieces of advice—learn to type, and don't learn to type. Most of them know how, and some have even taken a summer shorthand course, but none of them want to be secretaries.

The lucky ones slip into a filing or typing job in a desirable office—a friend of Daddy's got them the job, so they feel that someone up there will keep an eye on them and see that they are noticed in due course.

The intransigeants spend three months being turned down for editorial and copywriting jobs, and in desperation take the first secretarial job they can find. After all, the rent is due.

At this stage, the first wave of dropouts occurs. Many of the girls retreat to high-paid stenographer's jobs, on Wall Street or in big business, and decide to earn as much as they can and then

get out. Many decide that graduate school is the only answer—
the more degrees they have, the more they will be judged just on
their qualifications, not on their sex. Many get married.

The ones who persevere still hope that the companies that
hired them as secretaries will keep their promises, and that the
optimistic advice of parents and teachers will prove to have something in it. For the first few months, these lowly workers are
excited by their new status. Decorating the (shared) apartment
is fun, free evenings with no papers to write are fun, and now
they're in actual sight of the goal—surely it can't be too difficult
to take that last little step across the corridor?

They are fun to have around at first. The new bosses, scarcely
older than the secretaries, enjoy dictating to these glossy, eager
creatures, full of Proust and Nabokov and Cape Cod sun. The
secretary repeats the boss's gossip and shop talk to her friends,
who tell her how lucky she is to have such a marvelous job. She
does everything around the office she can think of, assuring her
boss that she just wants to keep herself informed about what's
going on and that she certainly doesn't expect overtime. Her big
hope is that she will be noticed.

After six months, she feels that she's mastered her job and is
ready to do more. She begins taking manuscripts home, if she
works for a publisher; trying her hand at some copy, if she is in
an advertising agency. All she asks is an opinion on her work
when the boss isn't too busy.

He gets in the habit of giving her more to do. She answers
some of his letters all by herself, she runs errands, she listens to
him when he wants to talk to someone about a new idea. She can
always be asked to stay late to finish a big typing job.

But she gradually realizes that this isn't getting her any closer
to what she had in mind. Now the crisis begins. She gets sulky,
petulant, overeager, bored. She begins to be late back from
lunch, to read at her desk. Her boss gets irritated, occasionally
lectures her about how to get ahead: "You have to prove that
you're good at *whatever* it is you're doing. No one's going to
promote you if you're lousy at the job you already have." He
forgets what an absolutely terrible salesman he was when he first
joined the company.

Meanwhile, his secretary fights with her roommates; she can't stand her old friends from college; her winter coat is worn out, and she's dying to get rid of her madras bedspread and orange-crate furniture. She often goes to the movies, reads paperback mystery stories, and sleeps more than ever.

This is the point at which she's most likely to give up any ambitions she ever had. She may change jobs, she may stay put waiting for something else to happen. She may move to a different city, get married, start a boutique with some friends—the dodges are endless, at least in theory. None of them will get her out of the trap she is in, but she doesn't know that yet. Nor does she quite realize that wherever else she looks for her satisfaction in life, it will never again be in the world of the work she once so desperately wanted to do. If she gives up on it now instead of fighting, every job will be an attempt against ever increasing odds. There will be younger girls around who have fought it through from the start, and her competitive edge will be gone.

There is only one thing that can save her at this point, if she doesn't have a really remarkable talent or skill: the interest and encouragement of a powerful man. And she is lucky, because she is in the only section of society where she is at all likely to meet such a man.

The pattern has been seen over and over again. Caroline Bird, Helen Gurley Brown, Letty Pogrebin—the women who started the reexamination of women's roles that began in the sixties— all pay tribute to the boss who started them off, who urged them to try things they didn't think they could do, and who promoted them out of secretarial jobs. They also praise the husbands who encouraged them instead of trying to curb them.

The newest Women's Liberation writers seem to have followed a different pattern: Kate Millett is a sculptor, Germaine Greer an academic. They picked fields where it would be harder to keep them down if they performed adequately, and where patronage wasn't necessary for promotion. This is certainly a more reliable method.

But the girls who looked to the office for their chances had to find some way to break through the layers of tradition and prejudice that would have prevented them from showing their talents, and the best way of breaking through was to find an enlightened boss. A few of them found him.

Anyone who has had an enlightened boss, or known one, tends to believe that they are more common than they really are. They say, "Anyone can do it if she puts her mind to it." They say, "if you're discriminated against, find a company that doesn't discriminate." As we have seen, this doesn't much help the girl who *is* being discriminated against. She doesn't know whether other offices are different from hers. She knows that very few of them would admit to discrimination, and changing jobs could just mean another fruitless year finding out the worst about another company.

Worse still, she doesn't necessarily know that she is being treated unfairly. Certainly she is never told as much. She is told, "You can't expect to have everything all at once." Or "It takes a very special talent to be an editor, and a lot of flair and experience. Are you so sure you have it?" Her boss, if she pushes him too hard, might even snap: "You don't have my job because you're not as good as I am." She isn't sure exactly what's the matter or what's the truth. It is all too easy to make her mistrust herself and her still untried talents. Are they there at all? The things her English teacher praised her for now seem too puerile to remember.

She compares herself to the boys her age who are making twice as much money and being encouraged to try exciting new projects, and sometimes even being given secretaries. Maybe they *do* know more than she does. Her self-improvement projects fizzle out and leave her feeling worse than before. She depends entirely upon the good opinion of her bosses, which she knows she is losing through her boredom and distress.

By this time, some of the boss's criticisms have a sting of truth to them. She knows less than he, or even than a boy her age, because she hasn't been trained at all. No one has taken the trouble to explain much to her, because then she might get ideas above her station and refuse to do the typing. Instead, she has been subjected to frustration and humiliation that might well have demoralized an even stronger character.

Without encouragement from above, she won't have the confidence to challenge this implicit judgment of her. And if she doesn't keep her sense of possibility alive, she will begin avoiding work rather than profiting from it: she will see all the counsels of perfection ("Read the files. Understand everything that goes out of your office. Learn all you can about the firm and the industry.") as ridiculous irrelevancies or as efforts to get more work out of her. She will be cynical about the importance of the people she once admired and sought to emulate. She will debunk the firm—"How could they publish this rubbish? I'm dying to get out."

Barring a lucky break or sudden interest from above, her first two years at work will have spoiled work for her for good.

Perhaps she shouldn't be so vulnerable. Why doesn't she fight harder? She gives up awfully easily, doesn't she?

She *is* unrealistic and vulnerable, and she doesn't know how to cope with the situation, but then she has hardly been prepared for it. She has been told, "It's awfully difficult to get into journalism, you know," and "Women have a hard time getting anywhere," but she never quite realized what she would be up against. She has despised her trapped, boring mother, and vowed that she herself would never suffer the same fate. But she doesn't really understand why it happened or how to prevent it.

The values she was taught at school were all about freedom of choice, democracy, fairness, and effort rewarded. She learned to be ambitious and serious.

> Boys and girls sitting at the same desks, studying the same lessons, and absorbing the same standards alike learn that the two most respectable criteria for choosing one's life-work are that the work should have chances for advancement and that it should be "interesting."[1]

It's true that she learned typing and cooking while the boys learned machine shop, and that the high-school atmosphere of dating and football made popularity with boys more important than anything else, but she was not entirely dominated by the high-school scene. From a "good" home, with good aptitude tests and neat clothes, she was obvious college material and an obvious target for the teachers' interest. She could see that all the teachers, women and men alike, valued intellectual achievement. They warned her that whatever frivolous interests she might have now, they would cut no ice in the world of college and career. While the rest were cavorting at proms and games, she was storing up points towards the glorious future, when she would sail past all the mundane people and preoccupations of her town and see something of what was really going on out there.

Going away to college was a big step in her life; it cut her off for good from the narrow-minded locals, to whom marriage was the only goal of a girl's life. It gave her a sense of achievement—even being admitted to a prestige college was such a mark of selection that you hardly had to bother actually going to it, except that of course she wanted to.

And at college, egalitarianism ruled—or at least it was supposed to. There were some things she vaguely noticed; for example, more girls than boys took English, and when it came to the fellowships—Wilsons, Fulbrights—doled out at graduation, the boys got far more of them. There were very few women professors. At a girls' college, there might not have been even these evidences of discrimination to notice.

A girls' college had some other peculiarities. Founded in the name of women's rights, and staffed by women for whom getting educated had been a real struggle, it was likely to be extremely high-minded. There was an aura of gentility about it, of the era when women's education was justified on the grounds that they were the guardians of culture and the doers of good works. The lady graduates were supposed to use their learning in an altruistic way, even if that only meant being enlightened wives and mothers.

Literary culture was therefore its specialty. Commerce was certainly never mentioned, and it was difficult to get any sort of grasp of politics, practical or theoretical—the kind of ferment that went on at some of the big universities was unknown there, although an occasional radical professor was invited to make a speech. The college was a little too far from the real world to have the kinds of connections that Harvard had with Washington, for example, or Berkeley with Cuba.

What it did have was a strong sense of its own excellence and importance, and of the value of its graduates. They were obviously destined to marry only the best men, to live in only the best places. If a woman did succeed in public life, it was understood that she would be a graduate of the college. But she would not have succeeded by hacking her way through the jungle of commercial competition or by competing with men. She would have been a public-spirited welfare worker or a political volunteer, and her government appointment would be made to show that the government did not discriminate against women.

Could a girl with this background hope to survive in any corner, no matter how relatively genteel, of the business world? Should she even be let out of the ivory tower on her own?

The unpretentious, unambitious New Jersey secretaries who could fight their way through subways and lunch crowds, save up for their weddings, and laugh it all off, had some real advantages over the too sensitive college girl. They could often survive long enough to move far past her in the career stakes.

The unique combination of arrogance and naïveté that an expensive education can give a girl is, however, not her only handicap. There is also the fact that she has been trained to be a different type of woman from the mothers and (probably) wives of the men she works for. Her strongest identification is likely to be with the heroes, male and female, of her education and not with the women in her own family. The only women likely to be included in her pantheon are those who somehow managed to escape the family themselves.

While she was learning that she was the equal of men, and that the whole question should not arise when it came to serious things like work or intellectual life, the men were not learning that they were *her* equals. At college, they hardly even thought about it—they had almost no women teachers, and many of them had no women in their classes either. They did not notice the few women in the books as avidly as did the girls. The women in their lives were mothers and girlfriends, and they vaguely expected that the girlfriends would sooner or later turn into women like the mothers.

The office reinforced their expectation that they would live mostly in a male world, peripherally served by women. It was the girls who noticed a sharp conflict between their expectations and the reality of life at work. Far from finding comradeship and equal chances, they found a rigid caste system with themselves, hitherto so proud, near the bottom. The men, who were now in the jobs they had been led to expect, did not quite realize what was happening to the girls. If they did, they were still anxious for changes in the system that would threaten their own newly won status.

To the girls, it seemed incredible that their former friends and companions turned so quickly into traditional men, wheeling and dealing and even dictating. The process happened so easily, with so little apparent struggle—why couldn't they themselves figure out how to do it? Had the men done it themselves, in some observable way, perhaps the girls could have learned how by watching them. But they were simply carried upwards by the momentum of the system, and the girls were left behind. There was no technique to emulate, no mastery to learn from.

The girls still did not believe that there was a conspiracy against them, or even any ill feeling or desire to put them down. And in a sense they were right. Individual men could not very well be blamed for a system they did not create. The assumptions about woman's role came in a cloak of moral justification—men earned the living to support women while they had babies, the business world was no place for a lady, men were grateful for the devoted help of their secretaries. Many men genuinely believed these arguments; many more had simply never thought about it.

So the girls were left facing an impossible situation, in which they had to give up either their belief in themselves or their faith in the system.

The ones who gave up the former are familiar enough. They married and dropped out, like most working women. They may have minded it more than most, to the extent of suffering from Betty Friedan's "problem that has no name" as they stood over the kitchen sink. They may have tried to get back to work from time to time, with each effort accepting something a little more menial and marginal than before.

The ones who gave up on the system are newer. It took a whole climate of giving up by all kinds of people—students, blacks, former liberals—to make them see it that way, and to reinforce their suspicion that it might not be all their own fault. They were unsure enough to wait until many other people had criticized some of the things they didn't like—the autocratic power of management, the manipulation of employees, the strongly enforced rituals of organization life—before they moved to try and make things better for themselves.

It is a familiar story by now how Women's Liberation was born in the New Left, and abandoned the coffeepots and typewriters of the Movement to strike out on its own. The heroes of the revolution were behaving just like ordinary men everywhere, and the women finally caught onto the fact that no one was going to liberate them but themselves.

In common with the rest of the Charles Reich generation, a lot of these women simply dropped out. The office was the symbol of all that was most hated about the system—faceless, dead, mechanical, the bastion of exploitative big business and the home of its most boringly conformist servants—the indictment is familiar enough. No one, it was said, should be there, much less a woman who was doubly exploited: as an employee and as a female.

But as all of Charles Reich's critics have pointed out, saying boo to the office didn't make it go away. The girls who joined communes "cooked brown rice instead of Betty Crocker," as one of them pointed out; the girls who started their own cottage industries were doing the same thing as the housewives, society girls, and artists who had always played at shopkeeping when they didn't need or want real jobs. The girls in *Hair* were doing what actresses and entertainers had always done. In short, the Alternative Society offered no new roles to women, just dressed-up (or dressed-down) versions of the roles they already had.

Women's Liberation itself split into two factions, neither of which was much immediate help to the girls in the office. Betty Friedan's National Organization of Women (NOW) concentrated on legislative change, and the anti-sex-discrimination clause in the 1965 Civil Rights Act gave the reformers a powerful weapon.

Companies started being sued for discrimination, but it was notoriously hard to prove—the men who had always denied that they were being discriminatory continued to deny it. Maybe the girl wasn't good enough. There was plenty of competition for the kinds of jobs the girls taking legal action wanted, and some excuse could always be found for not hiring the girl. The expense and slowness of litigation were the companies' strongest weapons.

The more radical women were dissatisfied with NOW because it only sought to give women a larger share in the existing pie. Thus, it would benefit only a few women—those who could join the top men in exploiting the rest of humanity. Liberation for *all* women would only come when the class structure was completely eliminated, that is, after the revolution. It is hard to generalize about all the radical feminists, but a *New Yorker* profile drew a vivid portrait of one group, the "founding cadre."

> Unlike their reformer sisters, the radicals dismiss the system that they live in as a "male construct." Politically, at least in theory, they are "female separatists." Most of them came to the movement out of the student left of the nineteen-sixties, and they have lifted their own rhetoric from the rhetoric of radical politics. They identify with blacks, draftees, migrant farmers, and the Third World. In fact, they regard women as the true Third World of modern history. They read "the second class" for "the second sex," and they see their movement as the vanguard of the ultimate class war.[2]

This outlook gives them some obvious problems when it comes to changing the office situation. First of all, if it is only the ultimate class war that will change women's lot, then there is no assurance that it will ever change—belief in the inevitability of the revolution has, in America today, an abstract quality. It may be true that local, partial reforms like antidiscrimination laws will only help to make piecemeal gains, which will be eroded almost as fast as they are built up. But for most women, they provide the only obvious avenue to changes that will affect their lives while it still counts.

The radicals are also extremely critical of the ways women have tried to get ahead so far. Being supported by a man is out, obviously; exploiting sex, like a film star, is out; being a token woman, like Barbara Castle, is out; in fact, personal achievement of all kinds is suspect, as it prevents a woman from identifying with the feminist cause after she herself has made it. Most ambitious women would say that if they have to wait until all women can join them on the heights, then they don't want to be feminists; most other women would say that if there has to be a revolution to change their lot, they would rather have it unchanged.

For the feminists are not only contending with other women's feelings about feminism, but with their feelings about the left in general, their suspicion of educated women, and their distaste for the Alternative Society.

Most of the women in the office have come along a different road from the feminists. They have inherited the attitudes of their parents, their high schools, and the secretarial roles they now play. This gives them some of the feelings about the feminists that their class in general often has about the hippies and the New Left: un-American, unwashed, unregenerate. When secretaries say, "I'm not in favor of Women's Lib," they are saying, "I'm different from those girls. I don't understand or like them, and they have shown that they don't like me."

Their only contact with such women may well have been in the office, where they were either scorned and patronized by a woman who had made it, or annoyed by the attempts of a "radical" girl to enlist supporters for the cause. Neither one was likely to show much understanding or sympathy for the real issues in the secretary's life, and their solutions to office injustice seemed far-fetched—after all, these techniques hadn't worked yet, had they? The missionary attitude was met with blank refusal by the "heathen" secretaries to renounce their own idols and embrace the new faith.

It was no use for the missionaries to point out that the new religion offered salvation. To the potential converts, the new heaven didn't look at all like a place they would enjoy. Collective living, dirt, pop, pot—everything the media attributed to the new life-style was repellent to their conventional mores.

The unwillingness of most office girls to enlist themselves in the feminist cause weakens the efforts of all women's liberationists. But it is not their biggest problem. Far more serious is the resistance of the bosses. When a girl first discovers the feminist movement, her morale and cooperativeness at work suffer. Sometimes it starts as a pose—she feels that this is the way she ought to behave, even if her particular situation hasn't driven her to it already. Any friendly gesture seems like treason.

When she is derided for her new opinions, her worst suspicions are confirmed. They *are* male chauvinist pigs! They accuse her of humorlessness, but she can't see that there's anything funny about it. They say that her ideas aren't very original—but what does that matter if they're true? They tease her, they humiliate her in subtle ways, they stop taking her even as seriously as they did before. If they ever had any sexual interest in her, it evaporates. Even if she still looks the same, feminists are, by definition, stringy-haired Lesbians. Not that she would welcome their sexual attentions, she is so furious with them by now.

Almost worse are the men who sympathize, and thus make her feel that there is hope for change. It can be months or years before she realizes that for all their seeming good will, things haven't really changed at all—she is still doing the typing and fetching coffee, and they are still wishing her well. She has to learn, painfully, to judge the people around her by their actions.

No matter what attitudes she takes up at this point, she will have a hard time devising actions that can actually change the office scene and the deal she is offered there. She can take one of the traditional roads to success, if she is lucky, and this will get her out of her immediate bind as it has many women before her. If she is unsuccessful, she will either leave out of sheer frustration or become so demoralized that she gets fired. She has a cruel choice—either she sells out her principles or her boss. Neither alternative appeals to her.

By this time, she is disillusioned with the whole corporate scene. If she gets far enough into leftist theory, she renounces all interest in her job because she no longer wants to make it in the system. And a good thing too, because she has practically no chance of doing so. The more of a fight she puts up, the more her powerful superiors close ranks. The more radicalized she becomes, the more suspicious they are of her. Either she is dismissed as unserious and her pretensions are laughed off, or she is taken seriously—and eliminated.

If she joins an organization that shares her antiestablishment feelings, and tries to work against the people she has been fighting, she may well find the same situation that got her out of the New Left—women doing the typing. In any organization of more than about five people, the tendency for this to happen is almost irresistible. Even if it is composed entirely of women, and even if they decide to share the drudgery, the ex-secretary will be given the most. If there is a man in the organization, he will never quite realize just how much there is to be done, and he will be absent-minded about seeing that he does his share. The women will be too kind to point it out to him as often as necessary.

If the group is very self-conscious and aware of these traps, a rotation schedule may be devised, but it is excruciatingly difficult to avoid status comparisons, and the typing always lands on the low-status desks. Maybe one of the group left a better-paying job to do the work he believed in. Maybe he was brought in because legal advice or expertise of some other kind was needed. Maybe the time he can give to the group is limited. Any of these factors can work against the cleverest drudgery-sharing plan.

One small, left-wing research institute, which started out with the high ideals appropriate to its commitment to the "woman question," admitted that the problem hadn't been solved. "We now hire out the typing so that the same people in the office won't always end up doing it."

There is, in fact, a deep conflict between two of the goals of the girl who has been trying to revolutionize the office. One of her beliefs is that neither she nor anyone else should have to do the dirty work so that a boss or husband or son can advance himself. Each should do his own, and not climb at someone else's expense.

Her other belief is that she is entitled, by virtue of her education and talent and ambition, to a larger share of recognition than she is getting as a secretary. If these things qualify her for superior status, then someone who has more of them than she has is entitled to a better job still. Does she really believe in equality, or does she simply want the same gradations of inequality for women as for men?

Most women who have thought seriously about it realize that "office politics," like "sexual politics," is a question of power. For women to become powerful enough to change their status at the office, they will have to, somehow, become more powerful, so that they can make threats with real meaning. If all the currently dissatisfied women dropped out, how much of an impact would it have on the economy? on an individual firm? And how likely is such action? So far, the system has been able to brush off women's threats, because they have never been presented in a unified way.

Instead, divide-and-rule tactics have worked superbly. The women who have risen are used to the notion that the higher they go, the more "exceptional" will be their status—with all the rewards of praise and attention that this implies. Educated women are notoriously unwilling to lump themselves together with "a lot of secretaries," who will hold them back with their inadequate training and obsequious ways.

The secretaries, on the other hand, think, "If these women refuse the existing jobs and husbands, all the more for me!" Indeed, their stock goes up with some men as the polarity deepens between them and the feminists. They suspect that it might be even more profitable to play the role of "traditional" woman after the feminist revolution really gets going.

The educated women of the past did not really refuse to do the things men have come to expect of women—they simply demanded the chance to do other things as well. An "enlightened" man was one who "allowed" her to work *if* she made adequate arrangements for the children, saw that the house was well kept, and always had his dinner on the table on time.

The new feminism does try to change the behavior of men. It asserts that women will never have their share of the power unless men give up some of theirs; that women will never reach job equality if they do not have domestic equality. But so far, women have not found a way to change the men who are unsympathetic to their cause, or even to ensure change in the sympathetic ones.

There have been two alternatives open to the liberated woman—living with a man who shares her views and lives up to them (with all the risks of disappointment that this course carries) or abandoning the company of men altogether.

Although women do not yet have enough leverage to change the behavior of the recalcitrant, they are developing several potent weapons. The most powerful is the fact that as education has become a status symbol, so have educated women. They are more attractive and useful in the modern world than is the old-fashioned model. With all the irritations of having an ambitious secretary, it is hard for a man to go back to one who has never heard of his clients and contacts, cannot talk to them on the phone, and does not impress them. He himself gets used to the revitalizing chats with his intelligent girl.

There are advantages for him, too, in a more egalitarian work relationship, just as there are in a more egalitarian marriage. He can delegate more, and the output of his office or department rises in quality and quantity. The trick is to reap the benefits without letting the situation get out of hand.

Whatever he does, the ambitious girl is likely to leave him. Either he will encourage her enough to keep her until she rises, or he will frustrate her enough to drive her away. Either she will drop out, or she will take one of the upward paths that other women have blazed.

These paths are, by now, quite well-defined. Caroline Bird has identified them as:

> Dynastic women
> Women's women
> Token women
> Gimmick women
> Sex women
> Office wives and housekeepers

None of these escapes can be employed on a mass scale. The women on such a list are there to sell refrigerators to housewives, to focus attention on a particular job, to titillate and to surprise. Their *raison d'être* is their status as exceptions.

Many of these women have used the secretarial route to the

top. Those who have usually recommend it; after all, it worked for them. Those who had some other plan believe that if they had started as secretaries, there they would have remained.

In some fields, it is the only route there is for a woman to take. A student of women lawyers concluded, "A large proportion of lawyers in my study began as legal secretaries. Many obtained their own law degrees long after they were in fact independently handling legal work (although they did not have clients)."[3] The rationale for promoting a woman was often, predictably, her "special touch" with widows and orphans, or her finesse in divorce cases, which are frequently unpopular with male lawyers. A woman had a better chance if she came from the same social class as the male lawyers in the firm—the average secretary would have a hard time overcoming her multiple status handicaps, but the woman whose only handicap is her sex can go further because she is "one of the boys" in every other way.

The move out of secretaryhood usually has to take two directions—away from the office where a woman has served her secretarial term, and where she is still thought of as a secretary; and into a business that is smaller, less complex, and more easily managed than the one she knows about. She will have to find a fringe area, an unfrequented or undiscovered specialty left alone by the big companies.

Such women have to invent their own careers. A girl in fashion, for instance, will not start out by making anything done by the existing giant companies, but will perfect one very special sort of belt or scarf or eyelash. A real estate agent will find a small area of concentration, like flats for the mature single woman. Specialization and small beginnings are the imperatives for the girl starting out in business. She will have trouble raising capital until she has proved herself, and she will have a struggle to be taken seriously. But with all its drawbacks, starting up for herself and (possibly) being bought out when successful is a better way to crash the business world than leaping straight into its jaws as an employee.

No matter how high a girl rises in business, she will still feel some of the irritations that she felt as a secretary. She will never be free of people asking her just to type something out for them, just take notes at the meeting, or just sew on this button. She will always hear remarks about the unsuitability of women in business —if she protests that she is a woman, she will invariably be told, "Oh, I didn't mean you—you're an exception." She will be passed over for promotions, not given a drink after the meeting, not invited to the convention. She will not have as big an office as her male colleagues, no secretary (or not as many secretaries), a smaller expense account. The transition from secretarial to executive work will not solve all her problems by any means.

The men who previously encouraged her and explained things to her will now see her as a threat and a competitor, and she will miss their friendship. She will be weary of her struggles for equal pay. She will be afraid to take as much time off as the average man, and she will exhaust herself working harder than anyone else to prove that she is just as good. If she has a family, she will suffer agonies of guilt, which will be skillfully exploited by husband, in-laws, neighbors, housewives, and the children.

The biggest reason why so few women fight their way along the road to the top is that it is so difficult. Only a few think it is worth it to lead this kind of life. To the strains felt by the executive, male or female, are added all the special, almost insoluble, problems of being out of step with other women and yet not accepted as one of the men. The fact that any women tackle such a role at all is an index of the satisfaction they feel when they manage to bring it off.

The companies that promote women often do it because they suspect that their very femininity, their realism, and their knowledge of the housewife's world can be turned into commercial assets. This suspicion has often been borne out. Women have succeeded in appealing directly to female consumers, and in their efforts to prove themselves, they have often been more daring and inventive than men with a bigger investment in the status quo. The very fact that men can insulate themselves from reality behind the walls of success can impair their usefulness. Andrea Dunham, a copywriter who started her own advertising agency and, at thirty-one, expects to be a millionaire at forty, says,

> Most American admen have become dangerously isolated from social reality, and are ignorant of what really motivates ordinary people. They send doves into kitchen windows and white knights charging into suburban housing estates. . . . Is a soap powder really the most important thing in a woman's life? More important than the education of her child? Then why condescend to her by pretending that it is?[4]

With the same sort of realism, the girl who decides to make something of herself after a few years of knocking around offices can frequently plot a more sophisticated, deadly campaign than the average male job-hunter ever dreamed of. She knows the smell of a successful company and the unmistakable signs of a loser; she can package herself according to the tastes of the potential buyer; she has a wider range of acquaintance and anecdote to draw on than does the man who has stayed, happily, in one or two offices; and she can weave all this knowledge into an impression of great business acumen and worldly competence.

She trades on her status as an "exception." She is an unusual commodity, and as such presents no real threat to the man who hires her or to the colleagues who must work with her. She is an independent, who sells her skill and originality on the open market rather than climbing the usual corporate ladder.

Her great advantage is that her life has taught her to adapt quickly, to be opportunistic when necessary. She is quicker at spotting a trend and going along with it, whether it is the consumer movement, antipollution, or a new dress fashion, than are most bureaucracy-bound men after a few years of building an orthodox career. They are reluctant to throw out the methods that have worked for them so far; she knows that the only method that has worked for her is keeping a few steps ahead of the game, and she has no vested interest to protect.

She is like the old-fashioned capitalist entrepreneur; buccaneering and enterprising. She is always singled out by the "learn to type" school as evidence that their nostrums will work, and that great careers can be built from humble beginnings. But the nostrums have only ever worked for the very few, and their efficacy is being undermined today by the very people who purport to believe them.

It is, since the publication of such books as *The Organization Man* and *The Affluent Society*, a commonplace to point out that the very businessmen who talk the loudest about free enterprise, the open market, competition, and consumer choice are the very ones who think *their* trade should be protected by tariffs, *their* prices should be kept up by manipulation of supply, and *their* town is not big enough for another grocery store that would take trade away from them.

Similarly, the prophets of self-help, who tell secretaries that hard work and perseverance will get them whatever they want, have generally not had to struggle much themselves. Either they are secretaries who are satisfied with the jobs they are allowed to have, or they are men who have moved smoothly up the corporation career path. This path is mapped out quite clearly these days, and conformity is a more salable virtue than outstanding ambition. The secretary who did, at her level, what the organization man does at his would stay right where she is, just as he does —the difference is that she is standing on the ground floor, and he is standing on the escalator.

In any case, how many people have become Henry Ford or (to go back to the successful business girl) Mary Quant? They are household words simply because they are so rare. As Bernard Shaw argues,

> When some inconsiderate person repeats like a parrot that if you gave everybody the same money, before a year was out you would have rich and poor again just as before, all you have to do is to tell him to look round him and see millions of people who get the same money and remain in the same position all their lives without any such change taking place. The cases in which poor men become rich are most exceptional. . . . The rule is that workers of the same rank and calling are paid alike, and that they neither sink below their condition nor rise above it. . . . If we find, as we do, that it answers to give all judges the same income, and all navy

captains the same income, why should we go on giving judges five times as much as navy captains? That is what the navy captain would like to know; and if you tell him that if he were given as much as the judge he would be just as poor as before at the end of a year he will use language unfit for the ears of anyone but a pirate.[5]

It may be, generally speaking, a lie that self-help works, but it works just often enough to provide examples and ammunition for its prophets. The tradition of self-improvement literature— Samuel Smiles, Horatio Alger, Norman Vincent Peale—is familiar, especially in America, which did for a while provide more opportunity than the Old World for putting these ideas into practice. The notion that ambition, hard work, self-reliance, and the other pioneer virtues can carry a man to the top of society is an inherent part of capitalist mythology. It is the usual justification for great inequalities of wealth and power, and it is used as the opiate of the alienated worker. It has been strongly challenged by trade-unionists. In the thirties, most intellectuals stopped believing it. But for the last two hundred years, it has been the creed of most of the middle class.

The creed recognizes the existence of certain obstacles to success, but only those obstacles that can be overcome by the exercise of the virtues it preaches. Humble birth, physical handicaps, lack of capital, and absence of formal education are obstacles that can be dealt with, according to the creed, by the application of such qualities as Energy and Courage, Application and Perseverance, Thrift, Temperance, and Common Sense. Although the books do not expressly say so, White Skin, an Expanding Economy, and a Penis are other qualities that the heroes of self-help have in common. Obstacles that are not dealt with include depressions and prejudice.

This tradition is the source of most of the advice given to young men in books like *Get Ahead in Business* and *Up The Organization*. It is supplemented by more specific business advice. Typical is this list for "men who want to get ahead":

1. A successful manager watches the bucks. He recognizes the name of the game as "profits."

2. A successful manager takes risks that are consistent with his ability to make profits at the same time.
3. A successful manager understands figures.[6]

The application of this tradition to women is quite a new development. Most of the books aimed at secretaries were (and still are) simple manuals of secretarial procedure. Some were a bit more ambitious, and discussed *How To Be an Effective Secretary* in somewhat broader terms:

Show consideration for others.
Be pleasant.
Be humble.
Be appreciative.
Be attractive.[7]

Both of these books were written by executives of Manpower, one of the large employment agencies. The contrast in the advice they give to men and women is illuminating.

The advice to women is repeated in various forms in the other secretarial advice books, and the last point is usually the most important: "When I asked employers what they would like their secretaries to learn if they sent them on a course, 'How to make the most of their appearance' featured on many lists and 'To use deodorants' on even more!"[8]

These books do not even pretend to attack the question of rising from a secretarial job. Such a job is considered an end in itself. For many years, books like these were the only works available on women's place in the office. They were obviously no answer to the burning questions raised by the advent of the educated, ambitious secretary who wanted to get *out* of her job.

The Samuel Smiles school tackled this girl's problems by pretending that they didn't exist—or that if they did, they were easily solved these days. Robert Townsend's advice about changing jobs when faced with discrimination is typical of these easy answers. In fact, the Smiles-Alger tradition, true to form, has not managed to cope at all realistically with problems it was not designed to deal with, like sex prejudice. Its technique is to assert that its success philosophy, with a few minor additions, suits everyone.

This is true in a sense: if the advice is adapted too much to the recipient, the results are not likely to be the same. Telling men to watch the profits and women to use deodorants ensures that women will be disqualified from coping with the business world. They will end up being accused of thinking about deodorants when everyone else is thinking about profits.

The real questions facing the ambitious secretary were bound up with such basic things as changing sexual mores, class differences, and the whole point and value of work itself. The first writer to see the connection was Helen Gurley Brown.

Sex and the Single Girl, published in 1962, still had a touch of Horatio Alger. It emphasized individual effort and all the classical qualities: health food was added to Temperance; selective extravagance became an integral part of Thrift; but the rest of the list could stand pretty much unchanged.

But for the first time, two sets of facts were brought into focus together: first, that women faced special problems in the work world and had to deal with them in special ways; second, that success in work was important and rewarding for women and that anything less would leave them frustrated, no matter what lovely families they had.

Helen Gurley Brown did not confine herself to the "work hard and learn the business" kind of admonition. She attacked the central handicaps of working women: low status, the marriage myth, low pay, and sexual exploitation. She realized that secretaries could be kept in their places because they were younger and of lower class than their bosses. The reason they were younger was that the marriage myth hustled them out of the office before the years when they could reasonably begin expecting success. Their low-class status, reinforced by dead-end jobs and low pay, was one of the things that barred them from high-status jobs. Their dependence on marriage to get them out of the whole vicious circle made them sexually timid (a "bad reputation," with no career or class glamor to offset it, would disqualify them as marriage material), unwilling to compete at work, and thus ensured that they would remain secretaries.

Thus, she concentrated on two areas: helping girls to get through the prolonged period of singlehood that she (rightly) saw as a prerequisite to career success; and helping them to climb (or seem to climb) the class ladder, on the theory that if they looked and acted ready for a higher-status job, it would be harder to deny them.

Helen Gurley Brown herself did not master these feats thoroughly enough to endear her to today's liberationists, most of whom are snobbish about her. She rose extremely high and married extremely late for someone of her background, but her values (and even more, her tastes) are too philistine for the *New Yorker* readers who scorn her. But they all, without exception, read her secretly, which is a tribute to the extreme relevance of what she has to say.

Her advice on social climbing is the most interesting thing in her book. She recognizes the rigid nature of the American class structure, and she does not pretend that hard work and virtue will induce a man to marry or hire a girl across class lines. She says to the girl, first cross the lines on your own steam, and then he will marry or hire you. If hard work and virtue will help you to do this, then use them.

Most of her advice is extremely specific: Southern cooking is out; French cooking is in. Church, baby-sitting, Danish pastry, and sales are out. Serious books, wine, designer clothes, and money are in. The overneatness of the secretary must go: the bright lipstick, carefully set hair, and little tailored dress must give way to styles more subtle and relaxed. Lunches with "the girls," that staple of secretarial life, are out: self-improvement in the lunch hour, or being seen having lunch with an attractive man, must take their place. All these specifics will have changed a bit since the early sixties, but her general principles are still sound. Money is to be used to buy status, which often means using it in unconventional ways. Don't buy "necessities," she urges—far more necessary for you is the latest indispensable luxury. Emulate women who have the status you would like to have. Don't worry about marriage, because it is always available; but remember that the more you climb before marrying, the more desirable the man you will get.

The girls who scorn this advice do so for several reasons. Some are merely snobbish—they don't like the implication that *their* status could be improved. Aren't they already in the top 5 per cent of the population in terms of I.Q., length of education, father's income, and so on? The same girls, however, are busy complaining about their own jobs on the grounds that being a secretary doesn't match their views about their rightful position in life. If their status is so unassailable, why has it been attacked in this vital way?

Some complain that Helen Gurley Brown's goals are vulgar: surely there are nobler ends than high-powered jobs, big salaries, and glamorous husbands? If there are, and if the complainer is sincere, what is she doing reading *Sex and the Single Girl* at all?

More sophisticated girls might well object to the fact that Helen Gurley Brown, like others of her kind, does not answer the basic objection to the Alger myth: that it doesn't work for many. This is true of all the advice so far given to working girls. The liberationists are trying to provide more effective methods, but until their revolution shows signs of getting off the ground, the combination of social climbing and deliberate spinsterhood is probably as effective as anything else the frustrated secretary can devise.

Helen Gurley Brown's successor in the field, Letty Cottin Pogrebin, published *How to Make It in a Man's World* in 1970. Hers is a much less subtle book, repeating most of the old advice about hard work and devotion to the job. The interesting difference is that between the two authors. Helen Gurley Brown grew up in the Depression, never went to college, worked as a secretary for fifteen years, married at thirty-eight, and has no children. Letty Pogrebin graduated from Brandeis at nineteen and worked as a secretary for two years. She is married and has three children.

Letty Pogrebin's emphasis on the *business* side of business has been taken as evidence that the all-out sexy singleness of Helen Gurley Brown is out of date; girls don't need it any more to help them succeed. Look how much easier it is for girls to get the good jobs these days, and how much sooner they get them!

The return to "get ahead" platitudes really indicates that a girl with a prestige education has fewer barriers to cross to an executive job: it is, in fact, proof of Helen Gurley Brown's thesis. Few girls have ever leaped as many class strata in a single career as she has done, and the girls who do it today undoubtedly need all the heavy ammunition that she wheeled out. The Letty Pogrebins had an easier time, not because things had changed, but because of who they were; thus, their prescriptions are less radical.

The question of sex in the office is dealt with by all the advice-givers, to boost sales as much as for any other reason. Letty Pogrebin is against it (another instance of her conservatism), whereas Helen Brown is usually for it. But the consensus these days, except among the heads of secretarial colleges (who, like most of their generation, deplore the permissive society), is that it really doesn't matter. Sex is such a common commodity that it won't induce the boss to promote you, bother him enough to make him fire you, or notably change anyone's attitude towards you. Sleeping your way to the top just can't be done these days; there's too much competition. All that can be claimed is that working your way to the top is a surer way to get there, and that one of the fringe benefits of a prestige job is sex with prestige men.

It is also noteworthy that none of these books give the sort of detailed *business* advice that is found in the men's manuals. Appearance and behavior are, apparently, still the things a woman will be judged on; if she were judged on her competence, the advice would be directed to increasing it; and this sign would indicate that her battle for equal treatment had been won.

In the meantime, what all these authors are trying to deal with are the specific obstacles facing women in business. They fall into two very familiar categories: conflicting claims and prejudice.

The conflicting claims on women's time, housework and children, have provided the classical excuses for discrimination: the girls will inevitably leave to get married; they stay home if the kid has a cold; their husbands won't like it if they work; and so on. All the liberationists are tackling these objections, and the consensus now seems to be that indeed women will never achieve full job equality until the household tasks are also equally shared. Husband participation, community child care, and the rest of the program are all necessary to make sure that no employer can rely on his old excuses. The Pill and the population explosion have gone far to eliminate women's old slavery to childbirth; not only can she avoid pregnancy, but she *should* avoid it more carefully than she has in the past.

Prejudices may disappear when these obvious sources of inequality are eliminated; or so the optimists say. But it may linger inexplicably on. Indeed, it has remained a more potent force in business life than women's actual behavior has warranted, and there is no reason to believe that this will change.

The question is whether men are hostile to women inherently and irrevocably, or whether the hostility comes from the roles and relative status of men and women today. For of the hostility itself there can be no doubt. The critics of Kate Millett have pointed out that not all men are Mailers and Millers (or at least the heroes of their books), with their fantasies of female degradation, rape, and murder. But Germaine Greer asserts, with plausible evidence supporting it, "As long as man is at odds with his own sexuality and as long as he keeps woman as a solely sexual creature, he will hate her, at least some of the time."[9]

The workings-out of this hatred are various, and it is often difficult to tell whether a particular male attitude springs from such deep roots or whether it simply reflects the low status of female occupations in our society. For instance, Viola Klein mentions

> the complaint of an American professor about "the election by college women of the humanistic subjects in such numbers as to drive the men from those courses on the ground that they are 'feminine stuff,' thus depriving men of the liberal culture they greatly need."[10]

Nancy Seear, studying businessmen's prejudices, found:

> The proportion of girls in the science sixth in co-ed schools is no higher than in girls' schools, while the percentage of boys is markedly higher than in boys' schools. . . . In mixed

schools, some boys avoid the arts side not from a disinterested love of scientific truth, but merely to avoid working with girls or being taught by women.[11]

Frequently the men's attitudes are obvious results of their existing relationships with women. Vance Packard notes that women who trained as nurses in the big city hospitals, often in hopes of marrying doctors, found themselves the victims of ruthless sexual exploitation. "The medics seemed to expect the nurses they dated to obey their wishes just as they were required to do in the on-the-job relationship."[12]

The desire to *avoid* women is harder to understand, at least for a woman. The exclusive female responsibility for young children has been seen by many writers as one possible source of this hostility. It has been noticed that antipathy to "Mom" has been very strong in those suburban boys whose mothers made them the exclusive focus of their attention in childhood. In fact, the suburban pattern, with mothers and female primary-school teachers isolated with the children, is widely thought to have increased hostility towards women in children of both sexes. A Norwegian study cited by Packard concluded, "More boys showed immaturity where the father was absent... boys where the father was absent tended to react to their insecure masculine identification by compensatory displays of masculinity."[13]

An executive with this background is not likely to welcome female competition at work any more than he welcomed it at school. On the contrary, he is even more likely than most men to cling to any source of prestige and security that he can find. His "insecure masculine identification" may coexist with other sorts of insecurity; for, as Daniel Bell has remarked,

> Perhaps the most important fact, sociologically, about the American business community today is the *insecurity* of the managerial class. The corporation may have an assured continuity; its administrators have not. This is a consequence of the swift and remarkable breakdown of "family capitalism" and the transformation to corporate capitalism. The new class of managers, recruited from the general grab bag of

> middle-class life, lacks the assured sense of justification which the older class-rooted system provided. They have no property stake in the system; nor can they pass their power to their heirs. Hence the growing need of achievement as a sign of success and the importance of ideology as a means of justification.[14]

And hence, he might well add, the reluctance to relinquish such status trappings as secretaries. Sexual superiority is likely to become more, not less, important to a man with fewer other sources of distinction, as many observers of working-class marriage have noted.

Feminists are often warned that male hostility to women will increase as the women make career gains—in fact, that there will be a backlash. But if this hostility is innate, then it does not depend on women's status; and it will not change as that status changes. Women will have to force the hand of the men who hold the power. If the hostility does come from men's desire to dissociate themselves from low-status people, i.e., women, then things can only change for the better as women make gains.

There are other possible reasons, besides sheer prejudice of this kind, for the lack of feminist progress in the office. One is the time-lag caused by seniority. By the time a man ascends to a position of power, many of his ideas are already out of date. Management consultant Peter Drucker sees this as the biggest single problem facing business. The typical management mistake, he claims, is to try to rescue an obsolete product, that had its heyday in the manager's youth, instead of cutting losses and moving on to something new.

Thus, a generation of managers reared in the era of the old sexual ideology are likely to be unreceptive to change; and by the time more "enlightened" men take over the top jobs, the feminist girls will have given up in discouragement, the new managers will have absorbed the ways of their predecessors, and everything will go on as before.

But the men who have been most sympathetic to the new wave of feminism are unlikely ever to be in a position to bring it to the office. The gentle boys who renounce sexual superiority have also renounced corporate ambition, the rat race, selling out, and perpetuating the system. They have renounced for themselves the jobs that ambitious girls want; and they are likely to be replaced not by women, but by men with more traditional sexual attitudes.

The most egalitarian sex relationships are found among some professional couples, dropouts, artists, and others whose effect on mainstream attitudes is not likely to be very great.

Women cannot expect to win justice at work by depending on men's recognition of the rightness of their cause. They must find a way to bring it about no matter who objects.

Chapter Six

THE POOL PROLETARIAT

THE INVENTION OF the typing pool in the 1920's marked the biggest change in the conditions of office work since the first women were recruited. It fixed the operatives at a low-paid, mechanical level and made it more unlikely than ever that many of them would make a career in the office, or indeed stay in it any longer than they had to.

Office machines had been in use since the invention of the typewriter, still by far the most widely used one. The electric calculator came in 1906, and various electric recorders, sorters, and punchers followed it. The Hollerith card-sorting machine, one of the first of its kind, was invented to deal with the 1890 U.S. census. Had it not been used, it would have taken until the time of the next census, ten years later, to record the data.

Rather than the machines creating new office procedures, the machines themselves have usually been invented in response to a specific office need. This has been true even into the computer era —it was the U.S. census again that demanded new technology, and the first Univac was used to tabulate the 1951 returns. The new machine was a real miracle-worker: in 1960, fifty statisticians were able to do the amount of work that required 4,100 men in 1950.

The typing pool itself was, however, made possible by the invention of the dictaphone, which dramatically increased productivity. In one office, output per girl rose from thirty-one letters a day to ninety-two, and soon row upon row of dictaphone typists could be seen in almost every large company.

But new machinery was not the only impulse behind the streamlining of office procedure. "The rationalization of administration involves the establishment of standard procedures and the specialization of functions within the office. This does not necessarily involve the mechanization of work."[1]

A new breed of efficiency experts, full of American know-how and self-help philosophy, were trying to extend the successes of the Ford assembly line into every area of life. The king of efficiency experts was Frank Gilbreth, who not only showed how a machinist could make twice as many parts as before in the same time, but taught his dozen children to eat and take baths as efficiently as possible. The tone of Gilbreth's work is typical of the feeling about industrialism at the time: "It is a fortunate thing to be born in an age like the present, when the scientific spirit prevails in all fields, and where everything can be legitimately submitted to measurement."[2]

The man who applied Gilbreth's theories to the office was Frederick Taylor, "the father of scientific management." Taylor knew that the more data the managers had, the better they could manage. He also knew that offices were frequently the last bastion of inefficiency in a company—outmoded methods were clung to for prestige reasons, or because things had always been done that way and no one had bothered to think about it. Taylor showed that the processing of paper was like the making of raw materials into cars or cornflakes. He replaced the many individual decisions of an office day with a set of rules, and wherever possible replaced the clerks with machine operators.

But Taylor denied that his systems were anonymous or inhuman. On the contrary, he claimed that they simply got the routine part of the job out of the way faster, leaving everyone free to enjoy the benefits of more leisure and higher productivity. While engaged in the routine, the self-improving operative could be thinking up ways to improve her efficiency still further, spurred on by the thought of earning more and achieving a four- or even three-day week.

What happened, of course, was that the higher the output rose, the higher the company set the norms. Paperwork has proliferated as never before, and ways of dealing with it are more efficient than ever, but the four-day week is still a mirage. Efficiency itself does not do anything to improve the lot of the worker—

rather the contrary. Every improvement in technique means that the work becomes more routine and the profits higher. A pool typist turns out three times as many letters as an orthodox secretary; she is paid $110. a week instead of $155. A computer-puncher turns out hundreds more items than a typist; she earns $100. A part-time housewife works at maximum efficiency during her five-hour shift; she gets $2. an hour.

The machine, far from banishing monotony and exploitation, has spread them wider than ever before. The gulf has widened between the office workers and those who profit from their work. Marx's words to the First International in 1864 are more relevant than ever.

> In all countries of Europe it has now become a truth demonstrable to every unprejudiced mind, and only denied by those whose interest is to hedge other people in a fool's paradise, that no improvement of machinery, no appliance of science to production, no contrivances of communication, no new colonies, no emigration, no opening of markets, no free trade, nor all these things put together, will do away with the miseries of the industrious masses; but that, on the present false base, every fresh development of the productive powers of labor must tend to deepen social contrasts and point social antagonisms.[3]

It is not only a question of confining workers to mechanical jobs and denying them the political power to get out, or the technological power to organize things differently. It is also a question of presenting the system as something natural and immutable, and undermining people's ability to see it as something that man has created and that man can dismantle if it doesn't serve his needs. The machine operative is in a bad position to see his situation as a whole. One modern automation expert has said,

> Whereas the employee could formerly hope to rise gradually in the hierarchy through a number of intermediate stages, he now finds himself confined to the role of mere operator,

which not only fails to prepare him for more highly qualified posts, but makes it more and more difficult for him to adjust to situations requiring initiative.[4]

Today, the office is characterized at least as much by the typing pool as by the secretary. As the size of the office increases, the proportion of pool or mechanical workers increases too. For instance, in an accountant's office employing five girls, the pattern will go something like this:

1 receptionist-telephone operator
2 personal secretaries
1 shorthand-typist
1 bookkeeper-clerk

There are only two jobs that are largely mechanical, and all the jobs involve personal contacts and decision-making.

An advertising agency employing about twenty-five women might divide up the work as follows:

5 semiexecutives (pool supervisor, art buyer, possibly a lady copywriter or two)
5 executive secretaries
15 pool secretaries (each with responsibility for three or four men, but all doing copy typing and other large jobs as well)

This office is 60 per cent mechanized.

In a corporate head office with 150 female employees, the proportion of routine jobs climbs again:

5 supervisors
20 executive secretaries
10 receptionists
10 switchboard operators
70 shared secretaries, stenographers, pool typists
20 computer-punchers and clerks
15 miscellaneous (file girls, mail room, etc.)

Only one-sixth of these girls have jobs that are reasonably responsible and nonroutine.

The girl in the big firm, if she becomes an executive secretary, is, in some ways, very well off. She has most of the drudgery done for her; the files have special guardians and the typing is done centrally. But she is cut off from knowing about anything except the work of her particular executive, and so is even more surely at a dead end than is the girl in a small office.

For the men, the larger the office, the less drudgery of any kind they have to do. There is always someone around to fill in for them, and the responsibility is less than in most small businesses. Automation for them *does* mean, as Taylor promised, freedom from petty detail. And the fact that it creates a class of operatives with no hope of anything better does not concern the executives —their carpeted offices are miles from the computer room and the typing pool.

The large, automated office is often said to have become nothing but a paper factory, and this can certainly be true. Contact between worker and boss is minimized, workers are made as interchangeable as possible, and norms are established without consulting the girls who are to fulfill them.

No matter how mechanized office work becomes, it is still, in some important respects, different from factory work, and the differences loom very large in the lives of the women doing it. The basic economic situation may be roughly the same—propertyless workers selling their labor to capitalists who reap the profits it brings—but even at its lowest, the office has its advantages.

The traditional pride of the white-collar worker can be seen in his (or her) very title. He can wear street clothes on the job; he is not divested of his very individuality when he goes to work. The office girl spends a far larger proportion of her salary on clothes than does the factory girl, and this is a pleasurable source of escape.

One of the biggest complaints of factory workers is that they cannot set their own speed—assembly-line speeds are crucial matters of negotiation, and the sense of desperation induced by a speed-up has no counterpart in the office. Most of the machines there go only at the speed of the human operator.

> The number of office machines which subordinate the work of the clerk to the tempo of the machine, which take over the larger part of the discretion involved in the operation, and which require full-time, specialized attendants, is extremely small.[5]

Even the pools that have quotas cannot set a fixed pace, and the bursts of speed and slowness, varied throughout the day, are very important in controlling fatigue. The newest machines make life even easier for the operative. For instance, the electric typewriter increase output, not by enabling a girl to type faster, but by doing the hard work for her so that she gets less tired. The usual 20 per cent productivity increase after switching to an electric is the consequence of lessened fatigue.

The opportunity for human contact is immeasurably greater during the office day than on a factory shift—even where attempts are made to limit movement and conversation, they can never be as strictly controlled as in a noisy factory, where each person is fixed to her place on the line and cannot even hear the girl next to her.

The office is cleaner. The office is quieter. Its staff are usually treated with considerably more dignity than in the factory. Even though pay is no greater in the office, the fringe benefits, such as pension scheme and paid sick leave, are likely to be considerably more generous.

These differences were never dependent on the relative pay rates of the factory and the office, and they will not necessarily be eroded if that distinction ceases to exist. What will change the status of office work is actual change in its conditions. Already, some companies have moved their computer operations into separate buildings, in cheaper parts of town than those inhabited by the headquarters. Shift work, clocking in and out, fewer amenities, sometimes the wearing of an overall—it is no longer office work in the traditional sense, and the people who do it will come to have few of the traditional "office" feelings towards their work and their superiors.

Perhaps the companies that make these changes are storing up trouble for themselves. The identification of the office worker with his firm has kept him docile and subservient, in contrast to the wageworker who demands proof of his worth in his paycheck. If the office mentality goes, it will be a costly loss to the firms that have eliminated it.

Resistance to the pool has come from many sides and has often proved fatal to schemes for its adoption. The girls who are pooled miss the personal contact they used to have with the boss, and they dislike losing their hard-won shorthand skills. The day's work is more monotonous, since the pool typists are segregated from the secretaries proper and are confined to their own quarters and routine.

In fact, no one has pretended that the girls could be expected to like the new system. They are simply in no position to object. Some enlightened companies hold "discussions" with employees who are about to be pooled, on the misguided theory that informing them about the changes will head off their hostility. Other firms have found that turnover on the typist level is so fast that it is even possible in some cases to put only the new girls in the pool, so that no single employee has to change systems.

This technique has also made it impossible to assess the extent of unemployment caused by the changes in office technology. Whether it is a question of pooling, computerizing, or simply reorganizing, most companies can and do claim that there have been no firings as a result of the change. And office expansion has been such since the war that although the hiring rate may fall in individual cases, the job market has generally remained buoyant. When the Bank of America computerized in 1957, a vice-president claimed:

> new positions would be created by introduction of the computer system, and more than half of these positions would be at least four salary grades above the bookkeeping level, and those who held them would come from within the bank

through training and promotion. Although the vice-president did not say so, we shall see that employers were inclined to appoint men rather than women to the new positions of preparing programs for the computer.[6]

Unexpected objections to the pool system have come, too, from the men. The higher management enthusiasts for the new scheme all keep their own private secretaries, who can now devote themselves to pure ritual and deference while sending their own typing to the pool. But the middle men, who barely rated a secretary anyway, have lost one of their cherished marks of distinction.

Ingenious combination systems have been invented to deal with this problem, and with the lowering of morale that occurs in too regimented an office. In the semipool, the girls sit in a large room ringed by executive offices. Each does the typing and answers the telephone for two or three men, and the girls fill in for each other if their work load is unequal. This system keeps the advantages of the secretary's personal familiarity with her boss's work—she can answer his callers intelligently and interpret his handwriting—while gaining the efficiency of the pool.

But no company can avoid peaks and troughs of work; if there are enough girls to deal with the monthly statements, there will be too many unoccupied for the remaining weeks of the month. Staffing for the Christmas rush is either a last-minute headache or a question of relative idleness for most of the year. And to have a backlog of girls to fill in during sickness and holidays is obviously uneconomic.

The temporary system has grown up as a response to all these dilemmas. The classic use for temporary office workers has been to fill in during the summer holidays, but this is now being extended to cover every kind of variable work load, peak season, and rush time of day. The employment agencies have found that temporaries bring them higher profits—getting a constant percentage of everything a girl earns is more lucrative than getting one flat fee for finding her a permanent job. For the company, a smaller permanent staff is a great saving no matter how much they have to pay the temp.

Although many temporary workers are apparently women who cannot work any other way—they must have school holidays off, or move with an itinerant husband—it is an increasingly attractive scheme to girls who are bored, as so many are, with the usual office routine. The relatively high earnings and instant availability of temporary work mean that it can be combined with travel—either working abroad or in the form of three or four holidays a year. It provides a constant change of scene. And most sophisticated of all, it is a good way of looking for a permanent job.

Few girls, however, voluntarily do temporary work for longer than a year or two. They speak of the loneliness of it—although they are meeting new people all the time, the friendships that make life in the permanent office bearable do not have a chance to form. It is unsettling taking a different route to a different place every morning—far more arduous than a comfortable routine.

Germaine Greer has praised the temp system as a sign that women are learning to exploit the system that exploits them, and to refuse to give loyalty and dedication for a pittance. But the system is really an avoidance of the problem, not a solution to it. There is no chance of the temporary worker learning a business well enough to make a bid for more responsibility, and there is absolutely no job security. The temp is firmly placed as a second-class worker, immured in the routine paperwork, with little loyalty to a firm that has no responsibility for her.

At the moment, there is little danger of the temps putting the permanent secretaries out of work—in fact, the blandishments of the agencies, by increasing the supply of temps, have produced an even more severe than usual shortage of permanent staff. As in the office in general, the great growth in the temp ranks will have to come from married women presently not working, and they are indeed being strenuously wooed by the agencies. This will help to create an even further class distinction between the permanent girls, who will do progressively less of the routine work, and the temps who are brought in and discarded by the season.

The temp system is far from perfect even for the employers, who have to put up with inefficiency, carelessness, unfamiliarity with the work, and even attempts to spin out a job to make it last a few more days.

In fact, every system devised to make the office more efficient has its drawbacks. Temps don't know the work; pool typists don't know the idiosyncrasies of the people they are there to serve. Permanent secretaries have to be paid when they are needed and when they are not.

The average typing pool, under normal circumstances, is staggeringly inefficient. The whole process of turning letters into data, churning out the answers, and separating the decision-making part of the work from the routine part, has produced some ludicrous situations. The more the office is systematized, the less amenable it is to human control in any form. Parkinson's Law works well enough in the old-fashioned muddled office, but in the new streamlined one it goes beyond a joke.

An astonishing letter to *The Guardian* told of getting a hand-written reply from the East Midlands Gas Board, with the printed note: "This information has been hand-written on a pre-printed form in order to expedite a reply and help to save typing and other costs."

The Guardian commented,

> A spokesman for the East Midlands Gas Board said that it was quicker, and more efficient, for a clerk handling an ordinary accounts inquiry to write a brief note on the pre-printed form than to send material to the typing pool. Similar systems are employed by other organisations, including the Inland Revenue.[7]

In spite of such straws in the wind, the effort to mechanize the office goes on practically unchecked. The biggest recent step in this direction is, of course, the introduction of the computer.

The computer, like the typewriter, did not put people out of work in any obvious way—instead, it created whole new categories of jobs. It is impossible to imagine today's credit-card, travel, and welfare-state industries without the computer. The number of bank accounts and stock-market transactions has increased faster than human workers could possibly deal with them, and here too the computer is indispensable.

The computer, again like all previous office technologies, was supposed to free the office slaves. Instead, it has created even more pernicious forms of slavery. It has brought into being a class of operatives and a class of technicians, and the more efficient and complex the machines become, the more sharply these classes are divided. The engineers, mathematicians, and whiz-kids who design the programs, advise management on using the generally new toy, and feed a company's data into it are male, and the traditional male monopoly of technical education has ensured that this will be so. Prejudice has not really mattered here—the field was expanding so fast during the fifties and sixties that anyone who could do the work was welcome, but girls with a traditional education were not ready to take advantage of the opportunity. Indeed, previous prejudice made new barriers unnecessary—while a woman could not attend Cal. Tech. or M.I.T., there was small chance that she would emerge as a computer scientist.

The large class of keypunchers, on the other hand, is almost entirely female, and in some places this has even become policy. The typists, already trained on a keyboard, adapted easily, and if a company could train low-paid girls to do the work, it was certainly not going to spend the money to hire anyone else.

The other side of the coin was that the need for people to staff the new centers opened opportunities to girls who would otherwise have had a hard time making it to the office at all. The computer companies trained the girls, as the early typewriter companies used to do, and such was the need of individual firms for keypunchers that they would often pay for the training. A girl who could not afford secretarial school could now learn a skill that would boost her out of the file-clerk or factory-worker class.

She did not have to conform so strictly to the usual office mores, either. Sequestered in the computer room, she could look how she pleased, and complicated rituals of deference were not required of her. Indeed, for the first time in office history, she could be black. Some companies even managed to tie in computerization with "equal opportunity" employment policies, getting credit for training and hiring underprivileged girls, and staffing their computer rooms cheaply, while not having to cope with unfamiliar notions like black receptionists. The number of nonwhites in clerical employment in the United States went up 77 per cent between 1960 and 1967, compared to a 23 per cent increase in white clerical workers. The office, during this period, made more progress towards integration than any other area of employment. Some of the credit for this must be given to the computer.

Whether this first step would lead any further remained an open question. The keypunch girl is extremely vulnerable to changes in the economic climate. New machines can make her training worthless, and she is even more tied to the big company and the big city than is the typist. Rumors are heard of her imminent replacement by an entirely "self-programing" computer. She is open to exploitation by computer training schools, not all of which are keyed to local demands or indeed fulfill the promises they hold out.

The trend that could hit her hardest is now beginning—a slow-down in the computer business itself. The miracle machine has demonstrated that it is as vulnerable to misuse as any previous office system, the difference being that it costs a great deal more than most. Where the computer takes over entirely, the result can be the comedy of errors familiar to anyone who has ever tried to get a telephone bill corrected or get his name off a mailing list. The first wave of enthusiasm has vanished and some companies are decomputerizing, while others are reexamining their plans to change over.

The trouble comes, say the experts, because nonexpert managers don't understand the machines. The managers say the experts don't understand the business. This deepening split in the business world between the technicians and the businessmen will be far-reaching in its effect. It is increasing people's tendency to ask whether the old-fashioned manager is really necessary—a tendency that, as we have seen, is spreading throughout the corporate world. Once the experts have elicited an answer from the machine, surely putting it into effect is just a routine matter? Surely "intuitive" decision-making is a thing of the past?

Either way, the slave at the keyboard is not the one who will be asked to take over. If it is decided that the manager is expendable, the technician will be elevated in his stead. And there is no sign that the new experts are more humble than their predecessors or less likely to claim special privileges and menial service. Indeed, their long training helps them to justify such claims.

The introduction of expertise into the office can erode the importance of routine jobs faster than anything else. The rationale is that training must be used, that each job has an appropriate level of training, and that these objective measurements are far more valuable than fuzzy on-the-job estimates of people's skill.

An example of how the new emphasis on training can affect the office is provided by a frightening book called *New Trends in Office Management*. It provides a picture of the new "expert" manager in action:

> The science graduate who remarked to the consultants that he had not taken a degree "to have his ability measured subsequently" was one person whose eyes were opened when studies showed that only 60 per cent of his effective time was spent on graduate functions; the other 40 per cent went on semi-skilled clerical work.[8]

The implication is clear: such a manager will be even more jealous of his time and brain power than the traditional executive, and even more contemptuous of the abilities of his subordinates. Only a graduate will be able to perform "graduate functions" in his office, no matter how much some nongraduate might have learned on the job. And the graduate will never lower himself to perform a "nongraduate function," even for the sake of efficiency.

He will continue to send everything to the typing pool, even if it is slower to do so. Even if Herzberg proves to him that his girls are capable of "using their own words," he won't let them unless it is appropriate to their station. His office will slip back into the era of feudalism, with rigid castes and estates.

The same mentality, with its narrow view of human potential, is still trying to apply the most discredited legacies of "scientific management" to the office. One stylish-sounding way of doing this is called Variable Factor Programing:

> In VFP, the number of visitors, visits made, telephone calls and breaks are recorded, so that if too much time is being spent on these activities the faults can be remedied. In fact, the British Aircraft Corporation removed telephones from certain areas where they were shown to be hindering productivity.[9]

This is the outlook that times and rations trips to the lavatory, cigarettes, objects on desk tops, yawns. It hasn't caught up with "motivation" and "job enrichment." It doesn't realize that its ways of making the office more efficient have all been shown to be counterproductive.

The split between the male executives and the female operatives has made the imposition of this kind of caste system even easier. The company can count on women to seek their satisfactions elsewhere when they get fed up at work, and thus impose conditions on them that the old-fashioned male clerks would have found it hard to stomach. The man who now holds the kind of clerical job commonly given to women is considered a failure by himself and everyone else—the look on the faces of the few remaining middle-aged bank tellers, surrounded by young girls, is very revealing—but most of the men who are left in the office can now call themselves executives. "One of the major features of the modern office—the employment of women in routine clerical jobs—has meant increased chances for male clerks because few women starting in the lower grades either choose, or are chosen for, promotion."[10]

Rather than treating this as a fortuitous stroke of luck for the men, it might be truer to say that "increased chances for male clerks" are one of the main reasons for the sex-typing of office jobs by male executives.

Now that more women have begun trying to choose promotion —even if they are still not often chosen for it—new reservoirs of untapped female pool potential have to be found. The traditional pool girl, young and unmarried and all but unskilled, is increasingly in demand for office work of all kinds, and the gradual lengthening of her education and the lowering of her marriage age have contributed to her scarcity. We have seen how the relative isolation of pool work makes it suitable for the previously unemployed—the housewives, the minorities, the old.

The pool almost never, these days, sees the girl who is destined for a high-level secretarial job. As such girls have become rarer, better paid, and more demanding, the gulf has increased between them and the women who have no choice where or at what rate they will work. As long as there are any captive women, there will be pools to take advantage of their economic helplessness. And no matter how many women so far have escaped such a fate, the vast majority have not.

Every time the office recruits a new group of women, it pretends that it is doing them a favor. As it gives them a larger share of society's routine work, and pays them ever less for doing it, talk is heard of social need, equal opportunity, and responding to demands.

Women have always come in and out of the job market in response to the needs of everyone but themselves—working during wars, laid off during depressions, at home when required there, at work when the family budget demanded it. The flood of housewives into the pools and computer rooms represents no change in this rule.

The argument that society will crumble if married women go out to work is scarcely heard any more—instead, the president of Manpower calls for thirty thousand housewives to join his temporary work force this year. The papers report, "The long-term interests of the economy demand an increase in the productive labor force and this, for the most part, can only come from married women not currently working."[11] And Vance Packard notes:

> In 1967 a number of giant corporations moved their headquarters from Manhattan to suburban communities, and one of the interesting explanations was that these corporations

were seeking to locate near large pools of alert young white-collar housewives.[12]

The feminist argument used to be that the corporations were against such a trend, because it was more lucrative to keep women at home as captive, full-time consumers. If this argument was ever true, and if women were brainwashed by the media into staying at home so that they would use more detergent, it is true no longer. Not only are housewives useful to the corporations as low-paid labor, but allowing them to go out to work can create new consumer demands. The system is adaptable enough to sell the working housewife a second car to get her to the office, expensive clothes, prepackaged foods to take the place of money-saving traditional cooking, household gadgets, children's summer camps—the list is endless. Also, a two-job family has more to spend.

Where it is to the system's advantage to bludgeon women about their traditional role is that it helps to keep them from demanding too much from work. The female employee must continue to look on her work as secondary, contingent, a luxury for the budget and a privilege for her. And there has been no attempt in the media to change this attitude; on the contrary, every effort is made to see that she stays docile and productive, and doesn't seek the sort of satisfactions that will cost her boss money.

A perfect example of this double-think is the following insurance company advertisement (the industry as a whole employs about 70 per cent women):

DEAR BREADWINNER
Sorry I laughed when you nearly fell downstairs this morning. Didn't mean to. You were right to be frightened. I was too when I thought of it. The children and I are totally dependent on you. Money would soon run out. Fixing the stair carpet is not enough. . . .

Running at the same time was an advertisement for a large bank. It began, "Because you're a girl, your ambition is sat upon . . ."

and urged girls to come to the bank to work, where they would have a chance of promotion—all presented in the most altruistic fashion.

The bank is a little more up-to-date in the attitude towards women revealed in its advertising, and one reason for this is that it has a different employment pattern. The proportion of truly routine jobs in the insurance company is larger, and they need paper-processors who do not expect much of the job. So they want women who are imbued with the traditional undemanding spirit; women whose vocabulary still includes the term "breadwinner." Their business also depends on the old-fashioned family —without dependents, what man takes out insurance?

Banks, however, still need people who can deal with customers and individual accounts, and as their volume of business grows, along with the number of branches, the need for such people expands. Salaries in banking are low—it is no longer a promising career for a man, and the banks have trouble getting the applicants they need. While their appeal to girls sounds liberated, it is really more of the same old story—no matter what happens to the family, their business will not suffer. It might even increase as women achieve economic freedom, since there will be twice as many banking customers as in the days when the man handled all the money.

The government bureaucracies, like the banks, have trouble filling their insatiable demands for labor. Because these are the jobs the ambitious don't want, they can afford to offer strict fairness in terms of promotion, hiring, allocation of shifts, and so on. Places like post offices get the casual, the itinerant, and the newcomers. There is often an atmosphere of easy give-and-take that is far pleasanter than the tension and hostility to be found in an office where the rewards are bigger, the requirements more stringent, and the pace faster. The post office can accommodate young and old, black and white, male and female, as well as all the people who simply don't want to join the rat race.

Working for the post office has become, in some parts of the United States, the classic way for a dropout to make a few dollars to keep going for months of inexpensive non-working life. More orthodox office jobs, like secretarial work, do not serve the same function for dropout girls. Although many take jobs they have no intention of keeping any longer than they have to (the girl in *Zabriskie Point* says, "I'm a secretary, but it's not something I dig doing."), the using of the system to finance a "real" life elsewhere demands too many compromises, adjustments, adaptations. The requirements of dress, behavior, attitude, and schedule are too rigid.

So there are advantages to the large, anonymous system that has so many drawbacks. A sort of contentment comes from not having to give too much in return for a job, from not feeling particularly involved with it.

Michel Crozier, in a study of six Parisian insurance companies, found "job satisfaction" higher the lower he went on the ladder.[18] The high-salaried underwriters said, "There's no future for me here; it's a dead-end job; I'm frustrated." They worried about promotions, status symbols, the future. The lowly *perforatrices* (a job so exclusively female that even the word for it is feminine), or keypunchers, said vaguely, "Sure I like it here...."

Confined in their ghetto, such women make a virtue of necessity in the manner of all ghetto inhabitants. An elaborate ritual of loafing and sharing builds up in the pool; friendships are intense and solacing. Gossip and daydreams are shared. Anniversaries of joining, birthdays, leavings, engagements are ardently celebrated, with noisy all-girl lunches at flashy but inexpensive restaurants—one cocktail apiece and a gardenia for the fêted. The generous spirit of the pool extends to help with work, concealment of faults, and covering-up to such an extent that it is often hard for the managers to sort out the efficient from the incompetent.

The office clique does help the girls to resist exploitation; demands for higher output may be met with blank refusal, and where the girls have established a pace among themselves, it can have the force of an immutable law. The girls are aware of what is asked of each of them, especially in offices where they are expected to share the work-load. If one girl is perpetually behind and has to be helped out, they may press for her to be given a permanent assistant, or alternatively for someone more efficient to be hired, depending on the girl's status with the gang.

The pool girls are neither particularly impressed by the men they work for, nor even particularly interested in them. The bosses appear as distant beings, descending occasionally and usually disastrously to upset the status quo. A younger man, with little of the authority of power behind him, can easily become an object of contempt and ridicule. Giggling, whispering typists have embarrassed many a young trainee or junior executive until he could hardly bear to confront them, and began surreptitiously typing his own letters.

If the women are to submit to male authority at all, any sign of weakness in its façade is a bad let-down to them. Their belief in the justice of the system that has put them where they are may be small, but any further erosion of it is unforgivable.

The indifference to the idols of success that is found on this level in the office is related to the dropping-out of the hippie generation, and it is just about as likely to present a serious challenge to the system. The hippie, of course, can drop in again any time he wants to; and he would say that those who serve the system while feeling ill-served by it are doing the wrong thing. But if all the pools, with the people who staff them, were to disappear tomorrow, would not technology rise to the challenge as it has so many times before? The powerlessness of these people stems from the fact that they are not really needed; things can go on just as well without them.

In the meantime, the pool at least represents a great sponge absorbing all the labor that cannot go elsewhere; it alleviates some of the worst hopelessness of the underemployed woman. It has provided a temporary solution to one of the nagging problems of postwar society, pointed out by Myrdal and Klein in 1956:

> Something must be wrong in a social organization in which men may die a premature death from coronary thrombosis, as a result of overwork and worry, while their wives and widows organize themselves to protest against their own lack of opportunities to work.[14]

It must be recognized that the pool solution to this problem, such as it is, is only temporary; that it redistributes some of the productive work of society in the direction of those who have previously been excluded from doing it, but it does not reward them properly for their added burden. Most sinister of all, the system of mechanized office work, with its deadening effect on those who do it, may make it even more difficult than ever for them to make any further gains.

Chapter Seven
CONCLUSION

THE SECRETARIAL ERA can be looked on as the time when men taught women about the business world. At first they said, "This is ours—you keep out." But when the knocking on the door became too insistent, and it was obvious that there was more than enough work inside to go round, they began to say, "OK—you'll have to do the typing and keep your mouths shut, but you can stay." To make it work, they had to divulge the secret of how it all operated—a secretary can't file the papers if the file is locked. Now they have a corps of fully trained women on their hands, who are beginning to demand admittance to the executive suite. They can't now say, "That wasn't part of the bargain"; some of them, at least, are going to have to move over.

Secretarial work has served its purpose in the long task of re-integrating women into the modern world. It has given them a look behind the board-room doors, it has taken them out of the house, and it has given them the beginnings of financial power.

At the moment, although secretarial work is still an opportunity for many girls, it is a trap for many more. And it is composed of all the various traps that women now complain about. The vicious circle is all too familiar: lack of education and training comes about because a girl is not expected to have to use such things; job opportunities are closed because of this lack; low earning power makes marriage attractive; and the existence of the dependent housewife confirms the theory that women don't need careers of their own.

The secretary has the power to get out of this trap, but she doesn't yet know how to use it. In fact, she is rarely aware of just how much power she has.

She is the first worker to take advantage of the fact that mobile, retrainable, versatile staff are increasingly in demand, even in this supposed era of specialization. The secretary can fit into any office, and learn the new techniques faster than the men, imbued

CONCLUSION

with old orthodoxies, who employ her. As one man mordantly observed,

> Create conditions in which a semi-literate adolescent can pick and choose and come and go as she pleases at take-home pay of 75p an hour, and there is no difficulty in believing that a very large number of girls will spurn the disciplines and routines to which many an educated City clerk must submit.[1]

The "educated City clerk," however morally admirable may be his discipline, has only limited usefulness in today's office world. He is the heir of the clerkly tradition described by Lockwood:

> ... The highly individual nature of business methods introduced him to a routine peculiar to the firm in which he started his career. . . . His maturing experience would be peculiar to his own firm, often highly valuable to his particular employer, but relatively worthless outside.[2]

The inflexibility of management is something that companies and consultants are constantly trying to overcome; but making use of the supposedly greater "practicality" of women is a solution that has occurred to few of them. The lack of training that has kept women out of top jobs is the source of their flexibility, and eliminating their disabilities may also eliminate their special usefulness.

The question that no one has answered so far is how women are going to overcome these handicaps, or move into better jobs faster than at the present one-by-one rate. "Consciousness raising," lawsuits, changing demographic patterns—all these things have helped, and will continue to help, but none of them is likely to provide a complete solution.

Is equality at work the right place to start? The sensible Swedes claim, in a 1968 report on the status of women to the United Nations,

A policy which attempts to give women an equal place with men in economic life while at the same time confirming women's traditional responsibility for the care of the home and children has no prospect of fulfilling the first of these aims. This aim can be realized only if the man is also educated and encouraged to take an active part in parenthood and is given the same rights and duties as women in his parental capacity.

In return, women must give up their automatic right to dependent status, and will be expected to contribute to economic and political life like anyone else. "The husband's traditional obligation to support his wife must be modified to constitute a responsibility, shared with her, for the support of their children." But for this change to take place, women must be able to compete on equal terms in the job market. Otherwise, the family's standard of living will fall when the husband starts devoting part of his time to housework and parenthood, and few families will voluntarily make such a decision.

We have seen some trends in the working world that may help to make female equality a possibility. The computer, with all its disadvantages, has at least begun to introduce shift work and decentralization, which will help to make the work patterns of both men and women more flexible. It has gone a long way towards bringing the housewife back to work. It has also, in a few places, brought the four- or even three-day week into being.

An American researcher found that the number of companies trying the four-day week quadrupled between August 1970 and March 1971, and she expects the number to continue to grow rapidly. This does not always mean a decrease in working hours —four ten-hour days often replace five eight-hour ones—but it almost invariably cuts absenteeism and raises productivity. And Paul Samuelson has said that this revolution could "redress the ancient curse of female drudgery" as men turn to housework.

Changing the sorts of jobs open to women is quite another matter. The women freed for part-time work, or returning after their children are in school, are still concentrated in the lowest-paid jobs, and this situation has not changed at all in recent years.

It is tempting to believe that simply removing the sex-typing of jobs would bring about a sweeping change. But all the evidence is against such a view.

Where men have been attracted to "female" jobs in the past, they have taken the ones at the top of the range and made things even harder for the women. Teaching is, again, the classic example: as educated men have become more plentiful and have turned against business careers, they have been attracted back to the secondary schools, and even the primary schools, that they abandoned to the girls over the past century. They are still in the minority as teachers, but most school principals are now male.

Men's return to teaching has meant increased militancy and thus higher pay for all teachers, male and female, and this is the other side of the argument. But secretarial work, in the higher reaches that are likely to attract the boys, has probably had its pay scale raised more by scarcity than it could have had from any amount of agitation. Low pay is not these women's immediate problem.

Where men are entering secretarial work, they are doing so at the top. Many German top executives have two assistants, one male and one female. The man, usually an executive trainee in his own right, handles matters of protocol (supremely important in the formal world of German business), administration, and personnel. The woman does the usual office housekeeping.

The Katharine Gibbs secretarial school has started a summer course for men—college graduates only. They will be aiming for good jobs in business, with secretarial work only a "foot in the door." And they will only go for the secretarial jobs that now represent real achievement for female secretaries—the $20,000-a-year personal assistant posts. The "creaming off" of these jobs into a separate, male category will make things much worse for today's aspiring woman secretaries.

Another trend in the breaking down of sex categories is represented by the telephone company, which has hired some male switchboard operators in the wake of the Civil Rights Act. Some of these boys are semidropouts, using the work in the way they have used post office jobs in the past. Others are interested in moving onto the executive ladder. They will undoubtedly find this easier than will the phone company's women. The dropouts, who have decided that low occupational status doesn't bother them, will have no more effect on the situation of their fellow-employees than do the boys in rural communes. Exempt from the male prestige game, their presence in the same room with the girls will not enhance the girls' prestige.

The only advantage to male interest in secretarial work is that it may lead people to reconsider the justice of sex-typing altogether. A boy who tried to get a job as a typist recounted his experiences in the London *Evening Standard.* He found the same kind of irrational prejudice on every side that women have found when applying for "male" jobs. All the classic responses were there—from "You would disturb the other typists; they wouldn't feel free to chat in front of you" (the reverse of the "they wouldn't feel free to swear in front of you" argument), to "It's not prejudice against men; it's a tradition for women."

Male unemployment may lead to further challenging of this kind of thinking. A boy leaving school has a much higher chance than his sister of ending up on relief, unable to find any work at all. He will not long tolerate answers such as that given by the phone company: "Our point of view for many years was that the job was best suited to women." This point of view, in the United States at least, is now legally untenable. It would be almost too much to hope that the men who challenge such barriers will do so in the name of justice, and not with cries of "Do you mean to tell me that girl typists get $100 a week while breadwinners are out of work?"

Even where discrimination by sex is not illegal, as it is not yet in England, it is being eroded by the death of the prudery that dictated the segregation of the sexes in general. Coeducational schools, earlier adolescence, and greater sexual frankness have eliminated some of the fear of unchaperoned contact between the sexes at work. The diehards in the matter are, predictably, the men who are used to spending their lives in exclusively male company. The London Stock Exchange, which is now almost alone in the City in admitting no women at all, is made up of public schoolboys who are notoriously unused to female company in any form. From school to club to regiment to office, they live in a totally masculine world, and their neurotic horror of women is pitiable.

The rise of the female executive is another development that may help to produce a class of male secretaries—it is already chic in some New York offices to have one. But this, like the employment of dropout boys in clerical jobs, is likely to be marginal in its effect.

The death of sex-typing will make it harder to rationalize the denial of executive jobs to women, but by itself it will not eliminate the practice. This can only be done, somehow or other, by the secretaries themselves.

The possibilities opened by the idea of concerted female action have been explored—and unexploited—ever since Aristophanes wrote *Lysistrata*. The mass refusal of secretarial labor could have much the same effect as a mass sexual strike of wives, and is, presently, just about as likely. Although visions of hordes of militant secretaries, sabotaging the files, leaking secrets, conspiring and disrupting, are pleasantly outrageous, nothing of the sort has happened yet. The woman who told the secrets of the Vehicle and General Insurance Company in England, and thus caused its collapse, did so to help her son get ahead in his business career. Embezzlement cases usually turn out the same way—she is supporting an unemployed husband, or wants to set her lover up in business for himself. Even the girl who put L.S.D. in her boss's coffee claimed it was a mistake—she mixed it up with an ordinary sugar cube. None of the possibilities of sophisticated office sabotage have been tried.

Women know that they have access now to every secret corner of the business world, and they use this knowledge when they make secretarial work a device for job hunting, husband hunting, or seeing the world. The potential of office women has also been realized by the City of London Fraud Squad, which recently hired eight women to help in fraud-prevention work. "Even as casual or temporary typists or secretaries they can gain information which a man could hardly hope to penetrate."[3]

When it comes to securing opportunities, money, and power for themselves, women are reluctant to put this knowledge to use.

The traditional way for workers to get a bigger share of the pie is, of course, the union. But it has not been much help to secretaries. Partly, they are concentrated in jobs that have never been unionized:

> In the white-collar and office field (banks, real estate, insurance, as well as the office forces of the large industrial companies), unions have failed signally. In plants where the blue-collar force is organized, the firm usually follows the practice of granting tandem wage increases to the office workers, so that the latter have no need or incentive to join a union.[4]

Unionization has gone further in countries where the public sector of the economy is larger than it is in America. In Britain, eight out of ten white-collar workers in the public sector are organized, but only one out of ten in private manufacturing.

Women are often accused of being hostile to unions in general, and it is true that the hiring of nonunionized women has often been an attempt by a company to undercut the wages of union men. But it might have been smarter for the unions to have tried to recruit the women, rather than simply vilifying them.

For there is no evidence that women doing the same jobs as men are any more reluctant to join unions. In fact, "the proportion of women in clerical unions is usually roughly equal to their representation in the field of employment which the unions seek to organize."[5]

Studies of white-collar unionism have shown that it flourishes in highly bureaucratized businesses; in fact, the more the white-collar worker is treated like a wage-worker, the more he responds like one by joining unions. Traditionally, he has felt (and has been led to believe by his employers) that he is part of management, in feeling if not in fact, and that he will be better off currying favor with the boss than by opposing him.

This feeling has been diminished by the growth of white-collar work and the consequent routinization of so much of it. These have certainly been the causes of the recent resurgence in white-collar unionism, led in England by the Association of Scientific, Technical and Managerial Staffs. The high-pressure advertising for A.S.T.M.S. plays on the clerk's fear that he is losing out in the wage race to the manual worker: "My tragedy is that I picked up a pen instead of a shovel" runs the somewhat disingenuous slogan.

The efforts of white-collar unions have been to win professional status for their members by becoming self-regulating, with standards for training and employment applicable throughout a field. They have also tried to limit access to the quasi-professions they organize, and this is one reason why they have not been, and will not be, of much use to the secretary who doesn't want to remain one. The journalism unions, for instance, forbid the delegating of journalistic work to secretarial staff; this is not countenanced as a valid training method, and the ban means that it is likely that newspapers will suspiciously ask a girl who applies for a secretarial job, "Are you sure you don't want to write?"

Secretaries are strongly discouraged by their companies from joining white-collar unions even where they exist. The confidential, exclusive, trusting nature of their work is given as a reason why they should not "divide their loyalty"—although the union doesn't try to recruit them in order to learn their bosses' business secrets!

Secretarial salaries have risen so fast in recent years that interest in unions as a device for winning pay increases has been small. Some militant women in America have been trying to introduce unions where none existed before, reasoning quite plausibly that if the company was so much against them, there must be something good about them. And indeed they do provide the first vestiges of job security, good working conditions, and fair salary scales among the really underpaid. They are probably a necessary first step in educating women to political action, getting them to take their jobs seriously, and making them realize the narrow limits of the company's concern for them.

But they aren't much good to the girl who wants to move out of her lowly job. She is often told that, of course, union membership will make promotion out of the question; she has identified herself with the workers against the management. But this is not the real problem—it is simply that promotion to the executive levels, which are almost never unionized, cannot be regulated by the union—the union's power stops at that point.

White-collar workers have been relatively apathetic about unions for this reason. The ambitious ones did not want to identify themselves with their present jobs; instead of joining their fellow-workers in a union, they wanted to distinguish themselves from their fellow-workers as much as possible. This is true these days of the ambitious secretary.

Secretaries have their own organizations, but none of these can be called unions. They are toothless and supportive of the status quo. The National Secretaries' Association is strongly reminiscent of the Girl Scouts—the same emphasis on duty, fidelity, loyalty. It describes secretarial work as a "service career," and makes it sound almost like working for the Red Cross. We have seen its manual, *Secretaries on the Spot*, with its emphasis on self-improvement, self-criticism, and blind obedience.

This sort of thing is scarcely likely to make the walls of General Motors come tumbling down.

We have seen that the agitations of Women's Liberation, valuable though they are, are likely to politicize the girls who engage in them right out of the office, leaving the old system intact.

What *should* the frustrated secretary do?

Professor Galbraith has advocated a Minority Advancement Plan which would outlaw discrimination against blacks, women, and Spanish-speakers in top jobs. There would have to be proportional representation all the way up the ladder, throughout

the reaches now monopolized by white, English-speaking men.
(This monopoly is 98 per cent in the private sector.)

> One of the plain lessons of the last 20 years is that where
> equality for blacks, other minorities and those so treated is
> concerned, good intentions are not enough. Nor is a serious
> commitment to reform which fails to specify the exact change
> to be achieved. Nor is any measure which does not have the
> force of law.[6]

This makes lovely reading. But the professor does not spell out
how this legislation is to be enacted in the face of inevitable
hostility from white male legislators, media executives, and
campaign contributors.

It is true that legislation, and constant work for its enforce-
ment, will be necessary for women to improve their position in
the economy. The Civil Rights Act has proved a more powerful
weapon than the men who passed it expected. A scheme like the
Minority Advancement Plan would be more powerful still. Those
who argue that you can't legislate away prejudice have been
proved wrong by the progress of school integration and voter
registration in the South—halting as such progress is, it would
not have happened at all without the law behind it. Martin
Luther King said that he didn't care how prejudiced the
Southerners were in their minds as long as their actions complied
with the law.

Those who argue that women's legislative gains have been
illusory are equally wrong. It has been said that equal pay will
lose women their present easy employability; there is no evidence for such a view. Taking the airlines to court to make them
remove the marriage bar for stewardesses did not make them
stop hiring stewardesses.

The prerequisite for the passage of really strong legislation is
that women and the other "minorities" must realize that they are
in fact the majority. Any device to raise women's political consciousness will help in this task. All the movements that we have
seen as inadequate on their own will contribute—trade-unionism,
Women's Liberation, housewives going out to work, removal of

sex barriers. Together, they may make the necessary impact.

The quarreling about which road to equality is the correct one only damages women's chances of reaching equality. The liberationists who say that women don't (or shouldn't) want "equal access to the world of the ulcer and the coronary" shouldn't make this assumption for any other woman. And unless such access is gained, what chance will women have of using their uniquely feminine qualities (the existence of which is postulated by such a remark) for the good of the world? It is all very well to say that political, "reformist" action should be secondary to changing men's consciousness (as a reviewer of *The Female Eunuch* sardonically remarked, presumably by mass brain surgery), but men will not listen to those who do not wield the economic power they respect so much.

The man who said, "Why should I listen to my wife? She's just a dumb little ex-typist" is one who will be made to listen when his wife is no longer economically dependent on him. As Art Buchwald said, "Show me a street cleaner making $50,000 a year and I'll show you someone with as much dignity as the President of the United States."

The "pragmatists," who see no further than fitting people into the system as it exists now, are on the run. One rarely hears these days views like those of ex-President Conant of Harvard:

> Equality of opportunity is one of the cardinal principles of this country.... Yet at the same time, no young man or woman should be encouraged or enticed into taking the kinds of advanced educational training which are going to lead to a frustrated economic life.[7]

This sounds suspiciously like Vorster's remark, "The black child must never look upon the green pastures where he will never graze."

It has been thought by many that the amount of challenging work a society had to dole out was so limited that most people must be prevented from aspiring to it. Today, there are two directly conflicting views—one is that more people than ever before are doomed to mechanical jobs, while decision-making becomes so complex that only a very few will be involved in it at all. The other view is that technology will free most people from drudgery of any kind, and the creative use of leisure and the invention of more democratic political forms will be mankind's biggest problems. The probable truth is that while the second set of occurrences is a possibility, it is one that will only be realized by the direct seizure of power by the people themselves. "On the present false base," to go back to Marx, technology will only enrich the owners and enable them to disenfranchise the rest more successfully than ever before.

In any case, it is not the routine element in work that frustrates the worker. Mills contradicts himself when he asserts, "There is no inherent prestige attached to the nature of any work; it is ... the esteem the people doing it enjoy that often lends prestige to the work itself,"[8] and, on the other hand, says, "In fact, the educated intelligence has become penalized in routinized work, where the search is for those who are less easily bored and hence more cheerfully efficient. ... Education, in short, comes to be viewed as a sort of frustrating trap."[9]

Even the most "creative" jobs are largely composed of frustrating drudgery, which is bearable if the worker's sense of the worth of what he is doing, and his control over it, is strong enough. The constant search for "executive talent," the cries that there are shortages of engineers, doctors, trained people of all kinds, coexist with assertions that most people must somehow be persuaded to work below their potential. The task of those who would seek to reform the office must somehow be to integrate these levels, and to resist present tendencies to exaggerate the gaps between them.

Herzberg, in his study of motivation, said, "Apparently, the feeling of growth in stature and responsibility is still the most exciting thing that can happen to someone in our society."[10] He identified the components of motivation as achievement, recognition, responsibility, advancement, and the work itself. The first three of these should be achievable by anyone, doing any job; the possibility of the fourth should also exist in any job;

and the fifth is, then, a reward that could be obtained by many more than have access to it now.

The move for women's equality at work, because it affects the bulk of today's routine workers, can help to solve these problems for all workers. Women's escapism and retreat from serious interest in their work has damaged our whole society and contributed in no small measure to one of its deepest sicknesses: "Alienation in work means that the most alert hours of one's life are sacrificed to the making of money with which to 'live'. ... Over the last forty years ... , as the 'idols of work' have declined, the 'idols of leisure' have arisen."[11]

The world of work will encroach on the lives of more and more women. Perhaps realization of their power will help them to think of ways to use it to make their work more satisfying, and to wrest from their employers the rewards that they should have. There will be no conflict between the women's battle and that of the other victims of capitalism; it is everyone's battle, and what the women win for themselves will benefit the whole society.

REFERENCES

Chapter One

1 Dr. Benjamin Spock, *Baby and Child Care*, rev. ed. Hawthorn Books, Inc., New York, 1968

2 *Boston Globe*, May 31, 1971

3 Robert Townsend, *Up the Organization*, Alfred A. Knopf, Inc., New York, 1970

4 Shulamith Firestone, *The Dialectic of Sex*, William Morrow & Co., Inc., New York, 1970

5 Francis X. Sutton, et al., *The American Business Creed*, Schocken Books, New York, 1962

6 Alva Myrdal and Viola Klein, *Women's Two Roles*, Humanities Press, Inc., New York, 1968

7 Robert Townsend, *Guerrilla Guide for Working Women*, McCall's, New York, 1970

8 *The Guardian*, November 5, 1971

9 Trudy Baker and Rachel Jones, *Coffee, Tea or Me?* Corgi, New York, 1971

Chapter Two

1 Alice S. Rossi, "Equality Between the Sexes: An Immodest Proposal," *The Woman in America*, ed. Robert Jay Lifton, Beacon Press, Boston, 1967

2 Ivy Pinchbeck, *Women Workers and the Industrial Revolution*, Augustus M. Kelley, Publishers, New York, 1930

3 Kate Millett, *Sexual Politics*, Doubleday & Company, Inc., New York, 1970

4 Elizabeth Faulkner, *Technology and Woman's Work*, Columbia University Press, New York, 1964

5 J. R. Dale, *The Clerk in Industry*, Liverpool University Press, 1962

6 Charles Dickens, *Dombey and Son*, Signet Edition, New American Library, New York, 1964

7 Viola Klein, *Britain's Married Women Workers*, Humanities Press, Inc., New York, 1965

8 Alva Myrdal and Viola Klein, *op. cit.*

9 National Manpower Council, *Womanpower*, Columbia University Press, New York, 1957

10 *Womanpower, op. cit.*

11 Vera Brittain, *Lady into Woman*, Andrew Dakers Limited, London, 1953

12 David Lockwood, *The Blackcoated Worker*, Allen and Unwin Limited, London, 1958

13 Lockwood, *op. cit.*

14 Arthur M. Baker, *How to Succeed as a Stenographer or Typewriter*, Fowler and Wells, New York, 1888

15 E. H. Butler, *The Story of British Shorthand*, Pitman and Sons Limited, London, 1951

16 Lockwood, *op. cit.*

17 Fred Hughes, *By Hand and Brain*, Lawrence and Wishart, London, 1953

18 Herbert L. Sussman, *Victorians and the Machine*, Harvard University Press, 1968

19 George Bernard Shaw, *The Intelligent Woman's Guide to Socialism*, Random House, Inc., New York, 1971

20 Hughes, *op. cit.*

21 Clara E. Collet, *Educated Working Women*, P. S. King and Son, London, 1902

22 Henry Mayhew (ed.), *London Labour and the London Poor*, Augustus M. Kelley, Publishers, New York, 1967

23 Collet, *op. cit.*

24 "Women as Civil Servants," *The Nineteenth Century*, September 1881

25 George S. Bain, *The Growth of White-Collar Unionism*, Clarendon Press, Oxford, 1970

26 C. Wright Mills, *White Collar*, Oxford University Press, 1953

27 J. B. Priestley, *Angel Pavement*, Heinemann Ltd., 1930

28 Priestley, *op. cit.*

29 Priestley, *op. cit.*

30 M. C. Elmer, *A Study of Women in Clerical and Secretarial Work in Minneapolis, Minn.*, University of Minnesota, 1925

31 Christopher Morley, *Kitty Foyle*, Faber and Faber, London, 1940

32 Virginia Woolf, *A Room of One's Own*, Harcourt Brace Jovanovich, Inc., New York

33 Mary McCarthy, *The Company She Keeps*, Harcourt Brace Jovanovich, Inc., New York

34 McCarthy, *op. cit.*

35 Rossi, *op. cit.*

Chapter Three

1 Jonathon Gathorne-Hardy, *The Office*, Hodder and Stoughton, London, 1970

2 Gathorne-Hardy, *op. cit.*

3 Simone de Beauvoir, *The Second Sex*, Modern Library, Inc., New York

4 *An Englishman's Desk Is His Castle* (pamphlet), G. A. Harvey, Office Furniture Ltd., 1970

5 Mary Ellmann, *Thinking about Women*, Harcourt Brace Jovanovich, Inc., New York, 1968

6 *Sunday Times*, January 24, 1971

REFERENCES

7 *Sunday Times,* January 31, 1971
8 Elizabeth Myers, *The Social Secretary,* Brentano's, New York, 1919
9 Thorstein Veblen, *The Theory of the Leisure Class,* 1905, Augustus M. Kelley, Publishers, New York
10 Veblen, *op. cit.*
11 Klein, *op. cit.*
12 Geoffrey Mills and Oliver Standingford, *Office Organization and Method,* Pitman, London, 2nd ed., 1968
13 Beauvoir, *op. cit.*
14 Juliet Mitchell, *Woman's Estate,* Penguin, 1971
15 Pat Mainardi, *Sisterhood Is Powerful,* Vintage Books, 1970
16 Mainardi, *op. cit.*
17 Myrdal and Klein, *op. cit.*
18 Colette, *Earthly Paradise,* 1966, Farrar, Straus & Giroux, Inc., New York
19 Mills, *op. cit.*
20 Christiane Collange, *Madame et le Management,* Avon Books, New York, 1971
21 Rossi, *op. cit.*
22 Herbert Marcuse, *One Dimensional Man,* Beacon Press, Boston, 1964

Chapter Four

1 Germaine Greer, *The Female Eunuch,* McGraw-Hill Book Company, New York, 1971
2 Figures from U.S. Department of Labor, Bureau of Labor Statistics, and U.S. Department of Commerce, Bureau of the Census
3 Sutton, et al., *The American Business Creed,* Harvard University Press, Cambridge, 1956
4 William H. Whyte, *The Organization Man,* Simon and Schuster, Inc., New York, 1956
5 Bruce Bliven, Jr., *The Wonderful Writing Machine,* Random House, New York, 1954
6 Esther R. Becker and Richard L. Lawrence, *Success and Satisfaction in Your Office Job,* Harper and Row, New York, 1954
7 Becker and Lawrence, *op. cit.*
8 Becker and Lawrence, *op. cit.*
9 Martin H. Perry, *So—You Want To Be a Private Secretary,* Remington Rand, n.d.
10 Perry, *op. cit.*
11 Perry, *op. cit.*
12 Perry, *op. cit.*
13 Perry, *op. cit.*
14 Perry, *op. cit.*
15 Perry, *op. cit.*

16 Richard Hofstadter, *Anti-Intellectualism in American Life*, Vintage Books, 1963

17 Hofstadter, *op. cit.*

18 Hofstadter, *op. cit.*

19 Marilyn C. Burke, *The Executive Secretary*, Doubleday, New York, 1959

20 Antony Jay, *Management and Machiavelli*, Holt, Rinehart & Winston, Inc., New York, 1968

21 Anthony Howard, *New Statesman*, August 26, 1971

22 C. Wright Mills, *The Sociological Imagination*, Oxford University Press, 1959

23 Anthony Powell, *Books Do Furnish a Room*, Little, Brown and Company, Boston, 1971

Chapter Five

1 Margaret Mead, *Male and Female*, William Morrow & Co., Inc., New York, 1949

2 "Profiles" (Feminists) by Jane Kramer, *New Yorker*, November 28, 1970

3 Cynthia Epstein, *Woman's Place*, University of California Press, 1970

4 *Evening Standard*, November 25, 1970

5 George Bernard Shaw, *op. cit.*

6 Aaron Scheinfeld, *Get Ahead in Business*, Award Books, New York, 1969

7 Elmer L. Winter, *How To Be an Effective Secretary*, Pocket Books, 1965

8 Dorothy Neville-Rolfe, *The Power Without the Glory*, Literary Services and Production Ltd., 1970

9 Greer, *op. cit.*

10 Viola Klein, *The Feminine Character*, Kegan Paul, London, 1946

11 Nancy Seear, *A Career for Women in Industry?* Oliver and Boyd, London, 1964

12 Vance Packard, *The Sexual Wilderness*, David McKay Co., Inc., New York, 1968

13 Packard, *op. cit.*

14 Daniel Bell, *The End of Ideology*, the Free Press of Glencoe, Illinois, 1960

Chapter Six

1 Lockwood, *op. cit.*

2 Frank B. and L. M. Gilbreth, *Applied Motion Study*, 1917

3 Quoted in Edmund Wilson, *To the Finland Station*, Doubleday & Company, Inc., New York, 1953

4 Ida Joos, quoted in *White-Collar Trade Unions*, ed. Adolf Sturmthal, University of Illinois Press, 1966

5 Lockwood, *op. cit.*

REFERENCES

6 Elizabeth Faulkner Baker, *Technology and Woman's Work,* Columbia University Press, 1964

7 *The Guardian,* January 1, 1971

8 Michael White (ed.), *New Trends in Office Management,* Business Publications Ltd., London, 1967

9 White, *op. cit.*

10 Lockwood, *op. cit.*

11 *The Guardian,* October 22, 1970

12 Packard, *op. cit.*

13 Michel Crozier, *The World of the Office Worker,* The University of Chicago Press, 1971

14 Myrdal and Klein, *op. cit.*

Conclusion

1 *Daily Telegraph Magazine*

2 Lockwood, *op. cit.*

3 *The Times,* March 23, 1971

4 Bell, *op. cit.*

5 Lockwood, *op. cit.*

6 *New York Times Magazine,* August 22, 1971

7 Quoted in C. Wright Mills, *White Collar*

8 Mills, *op. cit.*

9 Mills, *op. cit.*

10 Frederick Herzberg, et al., *The Motivation to Work,* John Wiley and Sons, New York, 1967

11 Mills, *op. cit.*